Bob Warden's **NINJA**™
Master Prep™ *Professional* Cookbook

150 Professional Recipes to RULE THE KITCHEN!™

Published by DYNAMIC HOUSEWARES INC

10 9 8 7 6 5 4 3 2 1

First paperback edition 2010

Author:
Robert Warden

Book Design and Food Photographs:
Christian and Elise Stella

Assistant Designer: Kelly Machamer

Manufactured in the USA

ISBN 978-0-9841887-5-8

TABLE of CONTENTS

RULE THE KITCHEN!™

The first time that I saw the Ninja™ Master Prep™ in action, I was taken aback. I watched in awe as an entire tray of ice cubes turned into soft, powdery snow in seconds. In the decades that I've been working with just about every kind of kitchen appliance, device, utensil or gadget; I had never seen anything that powerful, yet so compact. I was staring into the fluffy white snow, and I was imagining the possibilities. Today, I am even more astonished by the Ninja™ Master Prep™ Professional. With even more power and double the speed, the Ninja™ Master Prep™ Professional is ready for any kitchen task!

With the Ninja™ Master Prep™ Professional's unique Ninja Blade Technology, it's not only powerful, but versatile. In just three split second pulses, the same machine that can obliterate a whole tray of ice cubes can make a thick and chunky salsa that is evenly chopped.

The secret is in the Ninja Blade Technology. Quite simply, tomatoes chopped in a conventional machine will be liquefied before the topmost layer can even make its way to the blades, The Ninja gets the work done in half the time—and with delicate fruits or vegetables, time equals texture!

This is why the Ninja™ Master Prep™ Professional has become indispensable to me in my everyday meals. It's powerful enough to replace my three decade old meat grinder (that used to take up an entire kitchen cabinet, all to itself) and quick enough to whip the creamiest chocolate mousse for dessert. It's allowed me to spend less time chopping, dicing, mashing or mixing, and more time with family or just plain enjoying the simple pleasure of cooking—actually cooking.

To say the Ninja™ Master Prep™ Professional makes entertaining easier would be an understatement! No other machine that I know of can cater an entire party, from appetizers to the smoothest, thickest frozen smoothies or cocktails… with not a stray chunk of ice to be found.

With the interchangeable Master Pod, I can easily move from chopping pecans for Pecan Crusted Salmon (recipe page: 69) in the Master Prep™ Pro Chopper, whipping up a fresh batch of Thick and Chunky Guacamole (recipe page: 11) in the Pro Processor Bowl, to making The Best Frozen Margarita (recipe page: 96) in the Pro Pitcher in seconds. Because the Chopper, Processor Bowl, and Pitcher are all dishwasher safe, I can get right back to my guests without worrying about cleanup.

The recipes in this book were all specifically written and tested for the Ninja™ Master Prep™ Professional, but these are the same classic dishes that I've been making for as long as I can remember. Now, they're just fresher, and with a whole lot less elbow grease involved.

To get the most out of your Ninja™ Master Prep™ Professional, just remember these helpful tips:

❶ Pulse your way to your desired consistency.

The Ninja™ Master Prep™ Professional is meant to be pulsed in quick bursts and will actually work better and faster this way, than simply holding down the button. The stopping and starting literally jolts the food up and down to better mix and evenly chop. When the recipes in this book refer to pulsing in seconds, pulse on and off for the duration of those seconds for best results.

❷ Use uniform pieces of food.

While the Ninja™ Master Prep™ Professional does all of the hard work for you and is quite capable of chopping large pieces of food; mixing similar sized pieces of food at the same time, will give you the most even results. Don't forget, it's so easy to pop off the top that you can pulse uneven pieces in two stages: large pieces first and then the smaller.

❸ Bigger batches aren't always better.

When pulsing chunky or hard food, such as raw vegetables, try not to pack the Master Prep™ Pro Chopper, Pro Processing Bowl, or Pro Pitcher to the very top. The Ninja™ Master Prep™ Professional relies on a little bit of room to move the food around to give you the most even and consistent results.

With the amazing power and versatility of the Ninja™ Master Prep™ Professional, and all of my best recipes, brimming with hundreds of helpful tips; grab a tray of ice cubes, pulse into fluffy white snow and start imagining the possibilities.

-Bob Warden

APPETIZERS AND ENTERTAINING

DIPS

SALSAS

FINGER FOODS

Pro Processing **Bowl**

Herbed **Cheese Dip**

appetizers

This creamy cheese dip is a staple of my entertaining. The garlic and fresh herbs are an irresistible combination your guests won't soon forget. Just make sure you have plenty of crackers because a little goes a long way!

Directions

❶ Place Parmesan cheese, garlic, lemon juice, parsley, chives, basil and onion powder in Master Prep™ Pro Processing Bowl. Secure top and pulse in quick bursts until Parmesan cheese is almost grated. If starting with grated Parmesan cheese, pulse until herbs are finely chopped.

Shopping **List**

¼ cup Parmesan cheese
2 cloves garlic, peeled
1 teaspoon lemon juice
1 tablespoon fresh parsley
1 tablespoon fresh chives
1 tablespoon fresh basil
½ teaspoon onion powder
8 ounces (1 brick) cream cheese
salt and pepper to taste

Serves **6**

❷ Remove top and use a spoon to push mixture down, away from the walls of the Bowl.

❸ Add cream cheese, re-secure top and pulse in quick bursts for 15 seconds, until cheese and herbs are well combined.

❹ Salt and pepper to taste and serve immediately or cover and refrigerate for up to 4 days.

Just about any fresh herbs work well in this recipe. Try oregano or thyme in place of the basil or even 2 teaspoons of dried Italian seasoning if you're in a pinch. Low-fat or even fat-free cream cheese works great too for the best low-fat dip around!

Microwave **Spinach and Artichoke Dip**

appetizers

Trying this recipe for Spinach and Artichoke Dip will make you question why you ever paid a restaurant to make it for you, or why you ever paid a store so that you could bring it home and nuke it from a frozen package.

Shopping **List**

1 cup sour cream

8 ounces (1 brick) reduced-fat cream cheese

4 ounces Parmesan cheese

2 cloves garlic, peeled

½ teaspoon salt

¼ teaspoon ground black pepper

1 cup canned artichoke hearts, drained

1 package (10 ounces) frozen spinach, thawed

Serves **8**

Directions

❶ Place all ingredients in the Master Prep™ Pro Processing Bowl, artichokes and spinach on top. Secure the top and pulse 5-7 times until combined, but chunky.

❷ Carefully remove blades from Master Prep™ Pro Processing Bowl and microwave dip for 2 minutes, stirring halfway through.

❸ Serve as a hot dip for tortilla chips, garnished with a whole artichoke heart and grated or shredded Parmesan cheese.

Make your own flour tortilla chips for dipping by frying fresh tortillas in a lightly buttered pan until golden brown. While traditionally served hot, this dip works just fine cold as well... simply skip the microwave.

Pro Processing **Bowl**

Thick and **Chunky Guacamole**

You don't have to turn to a store bought guacamole when you can quickly and easily create this incredible, and more importantly, fresh dip that dates back to the time of the Aztecs. At least you don't have to get out an ancient mortar and pestle like the Aztecs did, just turn to the Ninja™ Master Prep™ Professional for all your guacamole needs and you'll be able to use this recipe that calls for a little bit of spice to add a big kick to your next Fiesta.

Shopping **List**

2 ripe hass avocados

½ of 1 onion, cut in half

1 jalapeño pepper, ends trimmed and seeds scraped out

8 cherry tomatoes

juice of 1 lime

¼ cup sour cream

¼ cup fresh cilantro

salt and pepper to taste

Serves **6**

Directions

❶ Cut avocados in half by inserting a knife down the center until it touches the pit, then carefully rotating the avocado until it is sliced through on all sides. Separate the two halves, remove the pit and discard. Use a spoon to scoop the meat out, tracing along the inner skin of the avocado.

❷ Place all other ingredients in the Master Prep™ Pro Processing Bowl, onion first and cilantro last. Top with the peeled avocado. Secure the Bowl's top and pulse 2-3 times for a chunky guacamole. Pulse a few times more for a smoother guacamole dip.

❸ Salt and pepper to taste and serve with tortilla chips or alongside fajitas and burritos.

The lime juice in this recipe will keep the avocado from turning brown. To keep the guacamole as green as it can be, you may want to drizzle some of the lime juice straight onto the avocado immediately after cutting.

Pro Processing **Bowl**

Mexican **Cheese Dip**

appetizers

Game nights, movie nights, or just sitting around and chatting nights; I have many fond memories of this dip being a part of them all. Everyone just can't seem to get enough, so make sure to keep enough ingredients around for seconds to keep the fun going!

Shopping List

1 cup sour cream

4 ounces (½ brick) reduced-fat cream cheese

4 slices processed American cheese

¼ of 1 onion

1 jalapeño pepper, ends trimmed and seeds scraped out

1 tomato, top trimmed off and quartered

½ teaspoon cumin

½ teaspoon salt

Serves **6**

Directions

❶ Place all ingredients in the Master Prep™ Pro Processing Bowl. Secure the top and pulse 5-7 times, or until combined, but chunky.

❷ Carefully remove blades from the Master Prep™ Pro Processing Bowl and microwave dip for 2 minutes, stirring halfway through.

❸ Serve as a hot dip for tortilla chips.

I prefer white American cheese in this recipe, but a one inch slice of a bricked processed cheese like Velveeta melts very well.

Pro Processing **Bowl**

Tuscan **White Bean Dip**

With their slightly nutty flavor, cannellini beans (a.k.a. Italian white kidney beans) make a superb base for a bean dip that is a nice change from the ordinary.

❶ Place all ingredients in the Master Prep™ Pro Processing Bowl. Secure the top and pulse for 10 long pulses, or until smooth and creamy.

❷ Serve with toasted or grilled pita bread, pita chips, crusty baked toast rounds or rustic crackers.

Shopping **List**

1 can (14 ounces) **cannellini beans,** drained

¼ **cup olive oil**

2 tablespoons lemon juice

2 cloves garlic, peeled

2 teaspoons fresh oregano leaves

1 teaspoon salt

½ teaspoon ground black pepper

Serves **6**

appetizers

Pro Processing **Bowl**

Classic **Hummus**

There aren't many dishes that go back in history further than hummus, and likewise there aren't many dishes that I've been making longer myself.

❶ Place all ingredients in the Master Prep™ Pro Processing Bowl. Secure the top and pulse in 10 long pulses, or until smooth and creamy.

❷ Serve with warmed, toasted or grilled pita bread, pita chips, flour tortilla chips, crusty baked toast rounds or rustic crackers.

1 can (14 ounces) **garbanzo beans,** drained

1 ½ tablespoons tahini sesame paste

2 cloves garlic, peeled

3 tablespoons lemon juice

½ teaspoon ground cumin

¼ teaspoon paprika

salt to taste

Serves **6**

Pro Processing **Bowl**

Roasted **Pepper Cheese Dip**

appetizers

Although they are completely different, it's amazing how much bell peppers have in common with tomatoes. Other than the fact that they both come in red, yellow and green, bell peppers are one of those ambiguous fruits, like tomatoes, that are really a fruit, but used as a vegetable… and also like tomatoes, they make a great base for "vegetable" dips like this one.

Directions

1 Place all ingredients in the Master Prep™ Pro Processing Bowl. Secure the top and pulse 8-10 times until well combined.

2 Carefully remove blades from Master Prep™ Pro Processing Bowl and microwave dip for 2 minutes, stirring halfway through.

3 Serve as a hot dip for tortilla chips, grilled pitas, pita chips, toasted bread rounds or vegetables.

Shopping **List**

1 jar (7 ounces) roasted red peppers, drained

¼ of 1 red onion

½ cup plain yogurt

½ cup mayonnaise

8 ounces (1 brick) reduced-fat cream cheese

4 ounces Cheddar cheese

2 cloves garlic, peeled

1 tablespoon Dijon mustard

½ teaspoon paprika

Serves **8**

Try caramelizing the onions in a sauté pan before preparing the dip for even more flavor. Add a few drops of chipotle hot sauce for a little more spice.

Pro Processing **Bowl**

Chunky **Olive Spread**

I have a feeling you'll find this recipe invaluable when you find yourself with a few nearly empty jars of olives taking up space in the door of your fridge. Of course, I also have a feeling you will like the flavor this olive spread offers so much that you'll quickly be filling that space right back up in preparation for your next batch.

Shopping **List**

3 cloves garlic, peeled

1 cup black olives, pitted

1 cup green olives, pitted

1 cup kalamata olives, pitted

⅓ cup olive oil

2 teaspoons lemon zest

¼ teaspoon ground black pepper

2 tablespoons fresh parsley

Serves **8**

Directions

❶ Place all ingredients in the Master Prep™ Pro Processing Bowl, garlic at the bottom and parsley on top. Secure the top and pulse 5-7 times, until chunky, but well combined.

❷ Serve with crackers or on toasted bread rounds.

Drain and add a small jar (4 ounces) of roasted red peppers to bring a little more color (and flavor!) into your next party. Sun-dried tomatoes are yet another great addition.

🏆 Pro Processing **Bowl**

Fresh **Tomato Salsa**

Preparing your own homemade salsas is one of my favorite ways to enjoy the difference between store bought and fresh. Most store bought salsas have been cooked prior to bottling so that they may sit on a store's shelf longer, and a lot of the texture of a freshly made salsa is lost. You just can't beat the fresh flavors and crisper textures found in a recipe like this!

Shopping **List**

½ of 1 onion, cut in half

1 jalapeño pepper, ends trimmed and seeds scraped out

2 tomatoes, tops trimmed off and quartered

juice of 1 lime

½ cup fresh cilantro

salt and pepper to taste

Serves **4**

Directions

❶ Place all ingredients in the Master Prep™ Pro Processing Bowl, onion first and cilantro last. Secure the top and pulse 2-3 times for a chunky salsa. Pulse a few times more for a smoother salsa or taco sauce.

❷ Salt and pepper to taste and serve with tortilla chips, tacos or burritos.

To make a quick and easy tortilla dip, add 1 batch of Fresh Tomato Salsa to 1 tub of sour cream (16 ounces). Stir until well combined and dip in!

Pro Processing **Bowl**

Salsa **Verde**

appetizers

This Mexican Salsa Verde (Spanish for "green") gets its name from, well, just how green it is! Don't let its color or more sauce-like texture deter you, this salsa packs some flavor that no fiesta should be without!

Shopping **List**

1 small onion, peeled and quartered

3 cloves garlic, peeled

⅓ cup fresh cilantro

1 jalapeño, end trimmed and seeds removed

1 tablespoon vegetable oil

1 teaspoon salt

1 can (28 ounces) tomatillos, drained

Serves **8-10**

Directions

❶ Place onion, garlic, cilantro, jalapeño, vegetable oil and salt in Master Prep™ Pro Processing Bowl. Secure top and pulse in 5 quick pulses, until vegetables begin to break up.

❷ Remove top and use a spoon to push mixture down, away from the walls of the Pitcher.

❸ Add tomatillos, re-secure top and pulse in 5-7 long pulses, until salsa is nearly smooth. Serve at room temperature or refrigerate and serve chilled.

This recipe is pretty mild, so if you like it hot simply leave the jalapeño's seeds (where most of its heat is found) intact. Add a second jalapeño to go even hotter.

Pro Processing **Bowl**

Cool Cucumber **Mango Salsa**

Y ou may be inclined to call mangoes a "super-fruit" after trying this flavorful and cooling Cucumber Mango Salsa, but what you may not know is that mangoes are actually considered a super-fruit based on their versatility and the fact that they are loaded with essential vitamins and minerals. This particular salsa is like other sweeter salsas in that it is great served with chips or with various grilled meats. I guess you could even call this a super-salsa!

Shopping **List**

½ **cucumber**
¼ **of 1 red onion**
1 mango, peeled and pitted
½ **red bell pepper, top trimmed off**
juice of 1 lime
¼ **cup fresh cilantro**
salt to taste

Serves **6**

Directions

❶ Rough chop vegetables and mango into 1 to 2 inch chunks to better fit into the Master Prep™ Pro Processing Bowl.

❷ Place all ingredients in the Master Prep™ Pro Processing Bowl, cilantro last. Secure the top and pulse 2-3 times for a chunky, chutney like salsa. Pulse a few times more for a smoother sauce like salsa.

❸ Salt to taste and serve with tortilla chips or as a refreshing contrast to spicy food.

When shopping for mangoes, be sure to pick one that is very plump. The long flat pit in a flat mango could account for almost half of the fruit. The skin of ripe mangoes varies in color from yellow to red and should have very little green present.

appetizers

Pro Processing **Bowl**

Sweet and Spicy **Pineapple Salsa**

Great as a dip, but also amazing with grilled salmon, chicken, or pork, pineapple salsa has always been the salsa I find myself making most often. Given the mood, I also recommend adding in some cooked black beans to your finished product for a gratifying and protein filled twist on this recipe.

Shopping **List**

¼ of 1 red onion, peeled

2 cups fresh pineapple chunks

½ red bell pepper, top trimmed off

1 jalapeño pepper, ends trimmed and seeds scraped out

juice of 1 lime

1 teaspoon sugar

¼ cup fresh cilantro

salt to taste

Serves **6**

Directions

1 Place all ingredients in the Master Prep™ Pro Processing Bowl, onion first and cilantro last. Secure the top and pulse 2-3 times for a chunky, chutney like salsa. Pulse a few times more for a smoother sauce-like salsa.

2 Salt to taste and serve with tortilla chips or alongside grilled chicken or fish.

Bob's Tips

While fresh pineapple makes a wonderful salsa, canned pineapple chunks will work fine, as long as they are drained well. Most grocery stores also sell quarts of pre-cut fresh pineapple chunks or rings in refrigerated cases in or near the produce department.

Pro Processing **Bowl**

Tomato and Basil **Bruschetta**

I could never quite figure out if bruschetta was the toasted, crusty bread slices underneath or the fresh Italian salsa on top, but now I know that it's actually the name for the combination of the two! These two bite appetizers are almost certain to impress.

Directions

❶ Preheat oven to 425 degrees. Bake bread slices, single layer, on a sheet pan for 8-12 minutes until golden brown and crunchy.

❷ Place onion, garlic, basil, parsley and olive oil in Master Prep™ Pro Processing Bowl. Secure top and pulse 5-7 times in quick bursts until onion and garlic begin to break up.

❸ Remove top and use a spoon to push mixture down, away from the walls of the Processing Bowl.

❹ Add tomatoes, re-secure top and pulse in 5-7 quick bursts or until tomatoes are chopped into small chunks. Spoon mixture onto baked bread slices and sprinkle with salt and pepper to taste before serving.

Shopping **List**

1 loaf crusty bread, sliced thin

¼ of 1 red onion, peeled

3 cloves garlic, peeled

8-12 fresh basil leaves

1 tablespoon fresh parsley

2 tablespoons extra virgin olive oil

2 tomatoes, tops trimmed off and quartered, and seeded

salt and pepper to taste

Serves **6**

Long and thin baguettes work best for bruschetta. Rather than boring discs, slice the bread at a 45 degree angle for longer, more oval shaped toasts.

appetizers

Pro **Chopper**

Marvelous Stuffed Mushrooms

appetizers

This may be going a little too far, but I consider stuffed mushrooms to be the perfect appetizer. They are bite sized, full of flavor, and easily customizable to match the event they are being served at. Trying mixtures of goat cheese or crab are good ways to complement a more formal gathering (see tip below).

Directions

1 Preheat oven to 375 degrees. Snap stems from mushrooms to create mushroom cap cups that are ready for filling. Place removed stems into Master Prep™ Pro Chopper.

2 Add shallot, garlic, parsley, lemon juice, salt, pepper and olive oil to the stems in the Master Prep™ Pro Chopper. Secure top and pulse 3-4 times until stems are minced, not mushy.

3 Heat butter in a sauté pan over medium high heat until sizzling and then add the minced stem mixture to the pan. Sauté for 2-3 minutes until stem pieces begin to brown.

4 Remove stem mixture from heat and stir in Parmesan cheese and breadcrumbs until well combined. Spoon an overflowing mound of the mixture into each mushroom cap and arrange on a baking sheet, single layer.

5 Bake for 8-10 minutes until mushrooms take on a light brown, roasted color. Serve hot.

Shopping List

15-20 large mushrooms, scrubbed
1 small shallot, peeled
2 cloves garlic, peeled
1 tablespoon fresh parsley leaves
2 teaspoons lemon juice
½ teaspoon salt
⅛ teaspoon pepper
1 tablespoon olive oil
2 tablespoons butter or margarine
3 tablespoons Parmesan cheese, grated or shredded
½ cup Italian breadcrumbs

Serves **6**

Bob's Tips Pulse 8 ounces (1 brick) of cream cheese, 1 tablespoon lemon juice, 1 teaspoon Old Bay seasoning and ½ cup of canned lump crab meat 2-3 times and fill the mushroom caps without sautéing for an entirely different take on Stuffed Mushrooms.

Pro **Chopper**

Quiche **Lorraine Cups**

appetizers

S erved fresh and warm, these bite sized treats are a great choice for your next gathering. Be sure to also keep them in mind as a unique way to start off a nice picnic in the park, as they can also be served cold.

Directions

❶ Preheat oven to 375 degrees. If using thin phyllo dough shells, pre-bake them for 6 minutes to crisp up before filling with quiche or they may get soggy and collapse.

❷ Place eggs, cream cheese, white pepper, nutmeg and salt in the Master Prep™ Pro Chopper. Secure Chopper's top and pulse for 8-10 seconds until well combined and frothy.

Shopping **List**

3 large eggs
2 ounces cream cheese (¼ brick)
⅛ teaspoon white pepper
⅛ teaspoon nutmeg
¼ teaspoon salt
8 chives
4 slices bacon, cooked
1 cup Swiss cheese, shredded
24 mini puffed pastry or phyllo dough shells, tart cups, or 12 homemade pastry cups (see tips)

Serves **12**

❸ Add chives and cooked bacon slices to the egg mixture and re-secure Chopper's top. Pulse 3-4 quick times to chop bacon and onion into small pieces and disperse throughout.

❹ Arrange tart cups on a sheet pan and place a small pinch of the shredded Swiss cheese at the bottom of each.

❺ Use a small spoon to fill each tart cup with the quiche filling from the Master Prep™ Pro Chopper, scooping from the bottom to ensure getting bacon in each cup. Bake 10-25 minutes (time will vary greatly depending on which cups used), until tart cups are golden brown on the outside and toothpick stuck into filling comes out clean. Let cool for 5 minutes before serving.

Bob's Tips

To make your own pastry cups: use prepared puffed pastry sheets (sold in a 2 pack in the frozen food aisle), unroll and cut into 3 inch rounds. Form the rounds around the inside circumference of a 12 cup muffin pan before filling with quiche filling.

Light and Fluffy **Deviled Eggs**

appetizers

A long with dishes such as my Marvelous Stuffed Mushrooms, recipe page: 23, I find that Deviled Eggs are a time-honored staple of entertaining. I highly recommend using this recipe for your next get together as the Ninja™ Master Prep™ Professional allows you to make the lightest, fluffiest Deviled Egg filling I've ever had!

Directions

❶ Cut eggs in half lengthwise and remove yolks, transferring them to the Master Prep™ Pro Chopper.

Shopping **List**

12 hardboiled eggs, shelled
¼ cup mayonnaise
¼ cup salad dressing (such as Miracle Whip)
¼ teaspoon paprika
⅛ teaspoon onion powder
½ teaspoon ground mustard
¼ teaspoon salt
¼ teaspoon pepper

Serves **12**

❷ Cover egg yolks in Master Prep™ Pro Chopper with all remaining ingredients. Secure Chopper's top and pulse 15-20 seconds until the yolk filling is fluffy and smooth.

❸ Use a spoon or pastry bag to stuff the yolk filling back into the hardboiled egg whites.

❹ Serve garnished with an additional sprinkling of paprika over top.

 If you like sweet relish in your deviled eggs, simply add a tablespoon after step 2 and pulse 1 quick time to combine. This is also a good time to add my personal favorite… cooked bacon.

BREAKFASTS

GRIDDLED

Perfect Pancakes 29
Homemade Corned Beef Hash 30
Crêpes 31
Sage and Apple Sausage Patties 32

BAKED

Homestyle Biscuits 33
Cranberry Almond Muffins 34
Banana Nut Muffins 35
Boldly Blueberry Muffins 37

SPREADS

Hazelnut Chocolate Spread 39
Strawberry Cream Cheese 40

Pro **Pitcher**

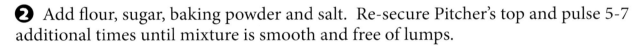

Perfect **Pancakes**

The original thinking behind this breakfast classic was to use up any ingredients that were considered luxuries or indulgences before Lent. Speaking of using up ingredients, I like to throw in any chocolate chips or any other sweet treats I may have laying around. See my tip below for instructions on how you can customize your own extra indulgent pancakes.

Directions

❶ Place egg, milk, butter and vanilla extract in the Master Prep™ Pro Pitcher. Secure Pitcher's top and pulse for 10 seconds, until mixture is frothy.

Shopping **List**

1 large egg
¾ cup milk
2 tablespoons butter or margarine, melted
¼ teaspoon vanilla extract
1 cup all purpose flour
1 ½ tablespoons sugar
1 tablespoon baking powder
½ teaspoon salt

Serves **4**

❷ Add flour, sugar, baking powder and salt. Re-secure Pitcher's top and pulse 5-7 additional times until mixture is smooth and free of lumps.

❸ Grease a griddle or nonstick pan with butter, margarine, or nonstick cooking spray. Heat over medium to medium-high heat until hot.

❹ Use the Master Prep™ Pro Pitcher's pour spout to pour about ¼ cup of the batter onto the griddle per pancake. Cook until top begins to bubble, and then flip. Let cook for 1 minute, and then use a spatula to lift side and check for doneness.

❺ Makes about 8 small pancakes or 4 large. Serve with butter and maple syrup, or fresh fruit and whipped cream.

 You can throw most anything into a pancake as soon as it is poured onto the griddle. Chocolate chips, blueberries, strawberries, raspberries, bananas and pecans—the ideas are endless!

Homemade **Corned Beef Hash**

Corned beef hash has certainly got to be an all time favorite way to use any leftover corned beef you may have. Serve it with eggs and some of my Homestyle Biscuits, recipe page: 33, for a traditional and hearty breakfast.

Directions

❶ Boil diced potatoes for about 2 minutes until soft, but not mushy. Strain and set aside.

Shopping **List**

2 large potatoes, diced small

3 cups corned beef, cooked

½ onion, peeled and cut in half again

¼ teaspoon garlic powder

¼ teaspoon pepper

2 tablespoons vegetable oil

Serves **5**

❷ Place corned beef, onion, garlic powder and pepper in the Master Prep™ Pro Processing Bowl. Secure Processing Bowl's top and pulse for 5-7 seconds, until corned beef is finely shredded.

❸ Add oil to a griddle, skillet or nonstick pan and heat over medium-high heat.

❹ Place cooked potatoes, and corned beef mixture in the pan and sauté, mixing only occasionally to allow time for browning. Cook until well browned, about 8-10 minutes. Serve hot.

Bob's Tips

If sautéing in a large pan, try using a spatula to push hash away from the center of the pan, creating a hole that you can fry eggs in. At the very least, you should definitely serve this hash topped with an egg, breaking the yolk into the hash before eating.

 Pro **Pitcher**

Crêpes

breakfasts

Essentially a thinner French version of a pancake, crêpes are best served with a filling of some sort, whether it be sweet or savory. I suggest trying them filled with my Hazelnut Chocolate Spread, recipe page: 39, and topped with Real Whipped Cream, recipe page: 142, for a rich and decadent dessert.

Directions

1 Place eggs, milk and vegetable oil in the Master Prep™ Pro Pitcher. Secure Pitcher's top and pulse for 10 seconds, until mixture is frothy.

Shopping **List**

2 large eggs

1 cup milk

1 teaspoon vegetable oil

¾ cup all purpose flour

1 tablespoon sugar

¼ teaspoon salt

nonstick cooking spray

Serves **4**

2 Add flour, sugar and salt. Re-secure Pitcher's top and pulse 5-7 additional times until mixture is smooth and free of lumps.

3 Grease an 8 inch nonstick pan with nonstick cooking spray. Heat over medium heat (no higher!).

4 Use the Master Prep™ Pro Pitcher's pour spout to pour about ¼ cup of the batter into the pan for each crêpe. Immediately after pouring, tilt pan from side to side to thoroughly coat the bottom of the pan with a very thin layer of batter. Cook until top is cooked and no longer sticky. Do not flip, let the heat cook though to the top instead.

5 Gently slide out of the pan to serve. Makes about 8 crêpes. Serve with your favorite fillings or toppings.

 Crêpes are great with almost any type of filling, even savory fillings like ham and cheese. When making crêpes for fruit or any type of sweet fillings, I like to add a small pinch of cinnamon to the crepe batter.

Pro Processing **Bowl**

Sage and Apple Sausage Patties

This recipe for an excitingly new take on ordinary breakfast sausage uses both the Master Prep™ Pro Chopper and Master Prep™ Pro Processing Bowl in order to bring out all of the unique flavors individually before they are combined.

Directions

❶ Place apple and green onions in the Master Prep™ Pro Chopper. Secure Chopper's top and pulse for 4-5 times, until apple is diced small.

❷ Add vegetable oil to a griddle, skillet or nonstick pan and heat over medium-high heat. Add apple and onion mixture to pan and cook for 5-6 minutes until apples are soft. Set aside and let cool for 15 minutes.

❸ Place sage leaves and fennel seeds in the Master Prep™ Pro Chopper. Secure Chopper's top and pulse for 5 seconds, until leaves are well chopped.

❹ Place pork loin, salt and pepper in the Master Prep™ Pro Processing Bowl. Secure Processing Bowl's top and pulse for 10-20 seconds, until meat is well ground.

❺ In a large bowl; combine ground pork mixture, cooked apple mixture, and sage and fennel mixture.

❻ Form mixture into 6 equal sized patties and cook on a griddle as you would any breakfast sausage, about 6 minutes on each side, using a spatula to press down until well browned.

Shopping List

1 apple, peeled, cored and cut into 6 slices
3 green onions
1 tablespoon vegetable oil
8 fresh sage leaves
¾ teaspoon fennel seeds
1 pound pork loin, raw, cut in 1 to 2 inch pieces
½ teaspoon salt
¼ teaspoon pepper

Serves **3**

When I make sausage, I always like to make it a day in advance, letting the raw sausage sit, refrigerated, overnight, for all of the strong flavors to really come out before cooking.

breakfasts

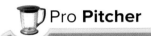 Pro **Pitcher**

Homestyle **Biscuits**

Considered a "quick bread" since it does not require extra time to rise prior to baking, biscuits are a great and quick addition to many dishes. Speaking of which, I find that these biscuits make a perfect side for my Homemade Corned Beef Hash, recipe page: 30.

Shopping **List**

2 cups all-purpose flour

1 tablespoon baking powder

¼ teaspoon baking soda

1 teaspoon salt

6 tablespoons butter

1 cup buttermilk

nonstick cooking spray

Serves **6**

Directions

❶ Preheat oven to 450 degrees.

❷ Place flour, baking powder, baking soda, salt and butter in the Master Prep™ Pro Pitcher. Secure Pitcher's top and pulse 5 quick times, just until combined, not smooth.

❸ Add buttermilk to the flour mixture and re-secure Pitcher's top. Pulse 5 quick times, just enough to combine.

❹ Flour a large surface and lay out finished biscuit dough. Stretch and lightly press dough down until it is well under an inch thick.

❺ Use a round cookie cutter or the rim of a thin drink glass to cut 12 biscuits from dough. Spray sheet pan with nonstick cooking spray and arrange biscuits, huddled together and nearly touching. Bake for 18-22 minutes, until tops are golden brown.

 The farther apart you arrange the biscuits before cooking, the crispier the edges will turn out. Arranging them close together like the recipe calls for will make extremely light and fluffy biscuits.

Pro **Pitcher**

Cranberry **Almond Muffins**

The sweet tartness of cranberries is perfectly complemented by the mellow nuttiness of its almond counterpart in this muffin recipe. For a variation on this recipe, try replacing the ½ cup milk with ½ cup orange juice for orange cranberry almond muffins that are a little sweeter and definitely fruitier.

Directions

❶ Preheat oven to 375 degrees. Line a 12 cup muffin pan with paper muffin liners or grease well to bake without liners.

❷ Place butter, milk, eggs and sugar in the Master Prep™ Pro Pitcher. Secure Pitcher's top and pulse for 8-10 seconds, until frothy.

Shopping **List**

½ **cup butter or margarine**
½ **cup milk**
2 large eggs
¾ **cup sugar**
2 cups all purpose flour
2 teaspoons baking powder
⅛ **teaspoon salt**
1 teaspoon vanilla extract
½ **teaspoon lemon zest**
¾ **cup slivered almonds**
1 cup frozen cranberries

Serves **12**

❸ Add flour, baking powder, salt, vanilla extract and lemon zest to butter and egg mixture in Master Prep™ Pro Pitcher. Re-secure top and pulse for 15-20 additional seconds until batter is smooth and free of lumps.

❹ Remove Pitcher's top, carefully remove blades and add almonds and cranberries to the batter. Use a wooden or plastic spoon to gently combine them into the batter.

❺ Fill lined or greased muffin cups with equal amounts of batter and bake for 25-30 minutes, until a toothpick inserted into the center comes out clean. Let cool for 5 minutes before serving.

If you have whole almonds in the pantry, simply give them 3 or 4 pulses in the Master Prep™ Pro Chopper before making the muffins to roughly chop them down to size.

 Pro **Pitcher**

Banana **Nut Muffins**

Some of my favorite breakfast memories are of my mother's fresh hot banana nut muffins right out of the oven. Bake up a batch of these warming treats to create a few memories for your family. You simply can't get something this good from any box.

Directions

1 Preheat oven to 400 degrees. Line a 12 cup muffin pan with paper muffin liners or grease well to bake without liners.

2 Place butter, milk, eggs, bananas and sugar in the Master Prep™ Pro Pitcher. Secure Pitcher's top and pulse for 8-10 seconds, until frothy.

Shopping **List**

½ cup butter or margarine
½ cup milk
2 large eggs
2 large bananas
¾ cup sugar
2 cups all purpose flour
2 teaspoons baking powder
½ teaspoon salt
½ teaspoon vanilla extract
1 cup walnuts, shelled

Serves **12**

3 Add flour, baking powder, salt and vanilla extract to banana mixture in Master Prep™ Pro Pitcher. Re-secure top and pulse for 15-20 additional seconds until batter is smooth and free of lumps.

4 Add walnuts to batter in Master Prep™ Pro Pitcher. Re-secure top and pulse 3-5 times, until walnuts are roughly chopped and dispersed throughout batter.

5 Fill lined or greased muffin cups with equal amounts of batter and bake for 25-30 minutes, until a toothpick inserted into the center comes out clean. Let cool for 5 minutes before serving.

 To make Banana Maple Muffins, reduce the sugar to ½ cup and add 2 tablespoons of pure maple syrup to the batter. Substitute pecans in place of the walnuts for the perfect complement to the maple.

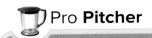 Pro **Pitcher**

Boldly **Blueberry Muffins**

A great thing about the Ninja™ Master Prep™ Professional is that it makes the idea of making your own homemade batters, such as this one for blueberry muffins, significantly less daunting. Sometimes it really does seem like it is worth it to use packaged preservative filled mixes based on their ease, but I think you might change your mind after trying this classic recipe for yourself!

Directions

❶ Preheat oven to 375 degrees. Line a 12 cup muffin pan with paper muffin liners or grease well to bake without liners.

Shopping **List**

½ **cup butter or margarine, softened**
½ **cup milk**
2 large eggs
1 cup sugar
2 cups all purpose flour
2 teaspoons baking powder
⅛ **teaspoon salt**
1 teaspoon vanilla extract
6 ounces blueberries

Serves **12**

❷ Place butter, milk, eggs and sugar in the Master Prep™ Pro Pitcher. Secure Pitcher's top and pulse for 8-10 seconds, until frothy.

❸ Add flour, baking powder, salt and vanilla extract to butter and egg mixture in Master Prep™ Pro Pitcher. Re-secure top and pulse for 15-20 additional seconds until batter is smooth and free of lumps.

❹ Remove Pitcher's top, carefully remove blades and add blueberries to the batter. Use a wooden or plastic spoon to gently fold blueberries into the batter, careful not to break them and release their color.

❺ Fill lined or greased muffin cups with equal amounts of batter and bake for 23-28 minutes, until a toothpick inserted into the center comes out clean. Let cool for 5 minutes before serving.

 Add a pinch of cinnamon to the batter for something a little different. Substitute fresh raspberries in place of the blueberries for homemade Raspberry Muffins!

 Pro Processing **Bowl**

Hazelnut **Chocolate Spread**

Let it be known that peanut butter and jelly sandwiches aren't the only way to enjoy a sweet, nutty spread filled sandwich! This decadent chocolaty alternative is not only superb on sandwiches, but also great on Melba toast or as a filling for Crêpes, recipe page: 31.

Shopping **List**

2 cups hazelnuts, shelled

2 tablespoons dark cocoa powder

¾ cup powdered sugar

4 tablespoons vegetable oil

Serves **10**

Directions

1 Place all ingredients in the Master Prep™ Pro Processing Bowl. Secure the top and pulse in long bursts for 2-3 minutes, until smooth and creamy.

2 Store refrigerated. Will keep for about 6 weeks.

 Once the prepared spread is finished you may want to add additional cocoa powder and powdered sugar to your own personal taste. You can also add additional oil for a creamier texture, re-pulsing until combined.

Pro Processing **Bowl**

Strawberry **Cream Cheese**

This recipe beautifully demonstrates how the Ninja™ Master Prep™ Professional can be great for when you want to quickly liven up something that is otherwise plain. For instance, with very little time added to your morning routine you can throw together a few ingredients that you probably have around, and easily go from having plain old cream cheese for your bagel to having a nice sweet treat!

Shopping **List**

1 cup fresh strawberries, tops cut off

1 tablespoon sugar

¼ teaspoon vanilla extract

8 ounces cream cheese (1 brick)

Serves **8**

Directions

❶ Place strawberries, sugar and vanilla extract in the Master Prep™ Pro Processing Bowl. Secure top and pulse 5-7 times, until strawberries are well chopped.

❷ Remove top and use a spoon to push mixture down, away from the walls of the Processing Bowl.

❸ Add cream cheese, re-secure top and pulse 5 times, until all ingredients are well incorporated. Serve on bagels or as a fresh fruit dip.

Bob's Tips — Any fresh berries or any combination of multiple fresh berries can be used in this recipe. A Raspberry Cream Cheese Spread is especially good and can even make a good, not-too-sweet frosting for all types of desserts.

LUNCHES

SOUPS

SALADS

BURGERS

Pro Processing **Bowl**

Cool and Creamy Gazpacho

This chilled Spanish soup is the perfect start to a cool meal on a hot summer day. Make a batch ahead of time and let all of the fresh flavors meld together in the refrigerator for an even better start.

Shopping List

1 Anaheim (mild) chili pepper, seeded and cut in quarters

1 cucumber peeled and cut in quarters

2 cloves garlic, peeled

2 tablespoons balsamic vinegar

1 teaspoon salt

3 ripe tomatoes, cored and quartered

croutons, for garnish

Serves **2**

Directions

❶ Place chili pepper, cucumber, garlic, balsamic vinegar and salt in Master Prep™ Pro Processing Bowl. Secure top and pulse in 5-7 quick bursts until pepper and cucumber begin to break up.

❷ Remove top and use a spoon to push mixture down, away from the walls of the Processing Bowl.

❸ Add tomatoes, re-secure top and pulse for 5 seconds, until all ingredients are well combined, but not liquefied. Serve chilled, topped with croutons.

Save even more prep time by substituting 2 cups of cherry tomatoes for the regular tomatoes in the recipe. I like to garnish gazpacho with both the croutons and a nice sized dollop of sour cream.

lunches

 Pro **Pitcher**

Roasted **Butternut Squash Soup**

I've always loved using butternut squash as a base for soup. The flavor is rich, nutty and slightly sweet, but what's best about butternut squash soup is its texture. Without any cream and only a little butter, the soup maintains a creamier consistency that makes this soup both savory and satisfying!

Directions

❶ Preheat oven to 425 degrees. Cut squash in half lengthwise, remove seeds and place flesh side down on a sheet pan. Bake for 35-40 minutes until flesh is extremely soft. Let cool before handling.

Shopping **List**

1 butternut squash (about 2 pounds)

½ cup baby carrots

2 tablespoons butter

3 cups vegetable broth

¼ teaspoon onion powder

⅛ teaspoon ground nutmeg

⅛ teaspoon allspice

salt and pepper to taste

Serves **6**

❷ Use a large spoon to scoop roasted squash out of rind, placing in the Master Prep™ Pro Pitcher. Add carrots, secure Pitcher's top, and pulse for 8-10 seconds until squash is smooth and carrots are minced throughout.

❸ Transfer mixture to a large stock pot over medium high heat. Cover with remaining ingredients and stir to combine. Bring up to a simmer and cook for 5 minutes.

❹ Salt and pepper to taste and serve immediately.

 Bob's Tips

Garnish with a dollop of sour cream to make this soup even creamier. Skip the onion powder, add 2 tablespoons of sugar and chill before serving to make a refreshing dessert soup that is best garnished with whipped cream.

Pro Processing **Bowl**

Cream **of Tomato Soup**

Are there any other soups that allow as much room for customization as a steamy hot bowl of cream of tomato soup? I certainly don't remember anyone ever topping their chicken noodle soup with things such as cheesy crackers, popcorn, avocado, or sour cream!

Directions

❶ Place all ingredients in the Master Prep™ Pro Processing Bowl. Secure Processing Bowl's top and pulse for 10 seconds in quick bursts until soup is nearly pureed.

Shopping **List**

¼ of 1 onion, peeled
2 cloves garlic, peeled
1 tablespoon fresh basil
1 tablespoon fresh parsley
2 tablespoons extra virgin olive oil
2 tomatoes, tops trimmed off and quartered
2 tablespoons tomato paste
½ cup heavy cream
½ cup chicken broth
salt and pepper to taste

Serves **2**

❷ Carefully remove blades from Master Prep™ Pro Processing Bowl and microwave soup, in Processing Bowl, for 2-3 minutes, stirring halfway through.

❸ Salt and pepper to taste and serve with Italian bread, or topped with croutons.

Bob's Tips

Substituting half and half for the heavy cream will keep this soup creamy without all of the fat. Try topping with a pinch of shredded Parmesan cheese for a little extra flavor!

Pro Processing **Bowl**

Broccoli **and Cheese Soup**

I have extremely little doubt that the mouth-watering flavor of this soup will be enough to make you fall in love with it. If for some reason it isn't, just keep in mind the high levels of fiber; vitamins C, K and A found in broccoli. But like I said, I'm sure the flavor would have been enough.

Directions

❶ Place all ingredients in the Master Prep™ Pro Processing Bowl. Secure Processing Bowl's top and pulse 5 quick times until broccoli florets are chopped.

Shopping **List**

4 ounces processed cheese (such as Velveeta)

1 cup frozen broccoli florets

2 ounces sharp Cheddar cheese

1 cup chicken broth

1 cup milk

½ teaspoon onion powder

¼ teaspoon white pepper

salt

Serves **2**

❷ Carefully remove blades from Master Prep™ Pro Processing Bowl and microwave soup, in Processing Bowl, for 2-3 minutes, stirring halfway through.

❸ Stir well, salt to taste and serve with crusty bread for dipping.

I've kept this recipe small to be microwaved straight in the Master Prep™ Pro Processing Bowl. The ingredients in this recipe can easily be doubled to make 4 servings, but must be made in the large, Master Prep™ Pro Pitcher, which is not microwave safe. In that case, simply heat on the stove over medium heat, until melted and hot.

Pro **Pitcher**

Cream of Asparagus Soup

I've always loved this soup full of bold flavors that only distinctively flavored asparagus can provide. Also, you may not know that asparagus actually has more vitamin C than citrus!

Directions

❶ Trim asparagus stalks about 2 inches up from the bottom and discard bottoms. Trim asparagus tips off remaining stalks and reserve. Finally, cut stalks in half.

❷ Heat butter in a large stock pot over medium-high heat until melted, and then add shallot, celery and garlic. Sauté until onions are clear and whole garlic cloves begin to brown.

Shopping List

1 pound fresh asparagus spears
2 tablespoons butter or margarine
1 shallot, peeled and diced
1 stalk celery, cut into 2 inch lengths
2 cloves garlic, peeled
2 cups chicken broth
1 teaspoon lemon juice
$\frac{1}{8}$ teaspoon nutmeg
$\frac{1}{4}$ teaspoon white pepper
1 cup half and half
salt to taste

Serves **4**

❸ Add chicken broth, lemon juice and asparagus stalks and bring to a boil. Once boiling, reduce to a simmer, and simmer for 15 minutes. Remove from heat, add all but 4 of the asparagus tips and let cool for 15 minutes.

❹ Place boiled asparagus and broth mixture, nutmeg and white pepper in the Master Prep™ Pro Pitcher. Secure the Pitcher's top and pulse for 10 seconds, until almost entirely smooth.

❺ Return the pureed mixture to the stove and cook over medium heat, stirring in the half and half, a little at a time. Stir constantly to ensure that the soup does not boil. Cook for 4 minutes or until hot and remove from heat. Salt to taste and serve each bowl garnished with 1 of the 4 reserved asparagus tips.

Bob's Tips

To cook the asparagus tip garnish in no time: fill a small, microwave safe, bowl with about 2 inches of water and drop asparagus tips down into it. Microwave for about 2 minutes or until water begins to bubble. Carefully remove from microwave and retrieve asparagus tips with a fork.

Cuban **Black Bean Soup**

This recipe for Black Bean Soup relies mostly on the beans themselves to bring flavor to the table. Of course, it also relies on my Fresh Tomato Salsa, but that can be substituted with 1 cup of any store bought salsa and two tablespoons of fresh cilantro.

Shopping **List**

2 cans (14 ounces each) black beans, drained

1 can (14 ounces) beef broth

1 cup Fresh Tomato Salsa, recipe page: 17

1 tablespoon lime juice

½ teaspoon chili powder

1 teaspoon cumin

salt and pepper to taste

sour cream, optional, for garnish

Serves **4**

Directions

❶ Place ⅔ of the black beans, and all of the beef broth in the Master Prep™ Pro Pitcher. Secure Pitcher's top and pulse for about 15-20 seconds, until smooth.

❷ Place a pot over medium high heat. Pour bean and beef broth mixture into pot and cover with remaining black beans, Fresh Tomato Salsa, lime juice, chili powder and cumin. Bring up to a simmer and then lower heat to medium low.

❸ Cook for 20 minutes, stirring occasionally. Salt and pepper to taste and serve hot, garnished with a dollop of sour cream.

 If you like spice, you may also want to garnish with slices of fresh jalapeño and you'll certainly want to consider adding a few drops of chipotle flavored hot sauce to the soup.

Pro Processing **Bowl**

Extra Creamy Egg Salad

This slight twist on egg salad gets its name from the fact that, by using the Ninja™ Master Prep™ Professional, the egg yolks are completely smoothed into the dressing for the creamiest egg salad possible.

1 Separate hardboiled egg whites from yolks by slicing in half and scooping out yolks.

2 Place all egg yolks, mayonnaise, yellow mustard, butter, celery salt and pepper in the Master Prep™ Pro Chopper. Pulse 5-7 times until yolks are pulverized.

Shopping List

6 hardboiled eggs, shelled

⅓ cup mayonnaise

1 tablespoon yellow mustard

1 tablespoon butter or margarine, softened

¼ teaspoon celery salt

¼ teaspoon ground black pepper

1 tablespoon sweet relish

Serves **4**

3 Add egg whites and sweet relish to yolk mixture and re-secure top. Pulse just 2-3 times until whites are chopped to your desired consistency.

Pro Processing **Bowl**

Ham Salad

Ham salad has always reminded me of growing up, as it was always my favorite way to enjoy the baked ham that was leftover after special family gatherings.

1 Place all ingredients in the Master Prep™ Pro Processing Bowl, onion at the bottom and sweet relish on top. Secure the top and pulse in quick bursts for about 5 seconds, until your desired consistency has been reached.

2 Serve in sandwiches or pulse extra fine and serve as a spread on crackers or mini toasts.

¼ of 1 onion, peeled

2 cups cooked ham

½ cup mayonnaise

1 teaspoon Worcestershire sauce

2 tablespoons sweet relish

Serves **4**

Pro Processing **Bowl**

Your Choice **Chicken Salad**

Chicken salad is one of my favorite things to make in the Ninja™ Master Prep™ Professional. It's not only easy, but depending on how many pulses you give it, the Master Prep™ allows you to choose a very coarse consistency with large pieces of chicken or a very fine consistency that could be used as a spread.

Shopping **List**

1 stalk celery, cut into 4 lengths

2 cups cooked chicken pieces

¼ cup walnuts, shelled

½ cup mayonnaise

½ teaspoon salt

⅛ teaspoon ground black pepper

¼ teaspoon onion powder

⅓ cup red grapes

Serves **4**

Directions

❶ Place all ingredients in the Master Prep™ Pro Processing Bowl, celery at the bottom and grapes on top.

❷ Secure the top and pulse in quick bursts for about 5 seconds, until your desired consistency.

❸ Serve in sandwiches, pita pockets, wraps or over a spinach salad garnished with diced apple and bleu cheese.

Dried cranberries make a great substitution for the grapes in this chicken salad for something a little different. Most grocery stores sell precooked "short cut" grilled chicken strips in their refrigerated cases, but I prefer to buy one of the store's whole rotisserie chickens from the deli when making chicken salad.

 Pro **Chopper**

Chopped **Salad**

I have a love / hate relationship with chopped salad! I love to eat it, but hate to chop all of the ingredients! However, the Ninja™ Master Prep™ Professional has now solved all of that, chopping all of these wonderful ingredients with ease. What I really love is the way that it chops the Cheddar cheese, giving it a real crumbled look that you could spend all day (trying) to replicate by hand!

Directions

❶ Place salad mix in a large serving bowl.

❷ Cut onion, broccoli florets, tomatoes, and Cheddar cheese into large, evenly sized chunks.

❸ Place onion in Master Prep™ Pro Chopper and pulse in 3-5 short pulses, just until chopped. Arrange in a thin line atop the salad. Repeat with the bacon, pulsing in the Pro Chopper in 4-5 short pulses and then adding to the salad. Repeat with the Cheddar cheese, pulsing in the Pro Chopper in 5-6 short pulses and then adding to the salad.

❹ Place tomatoes in Master Prep™ Pro Processing Bowl and pulse just 2-3 short pulses, just until chopped. Arrange in another thin line atop the salad. Repeat with the broccoli florets, pulsing in the Processing Bowl just 2-3 short pulses and then adding to the salad.

❺ Serve alongside Creamy Parmesan Dressing.

Shopping **List**

1 bag salad mix

½ of 1 small red onion

8-10 slices bacon, cooked

4 ounces sharp Cheddar cheese

2 tomatoes, seeded

1 ½ cups broccoli florets

1 batch Creamy Parmesan Dressing, recipe page: 137

Serves **4**

 Remove most of the broccoli's stems before chopping for best results. The sharper the Cheddar cheese, the better your results will be... as harder cheeses grate better.

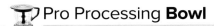 Pro Processing **Bowl**

Steak **and Cheese Burgers**

Though a burger is probably not the first thing you'd think to make with the Ninja™ Master Prep™ Professional, these burgers are extraordinary and may have you thinking... why didn't I think of that? No need to top—the cheese is mixed right in for a REAL steak burger that is literally bursting with flavor.

Directions

❶ Place sirloin chunks and Montreal steak seasoning in Master Prep™ Pro Processing Bowl. Secure Processing Bowl's top and pulse for 10-15 seconds, until meat is ground.

Shopping **List**

1 pound sirloin steak, cut into 1 to 2 inch chunks
1 ½ teaspoons Montreal steak seasoning
4 ounces Cheddar cheese, cut into 1 inch cubes
hamburger buns and fixings, optional

Serves **4**

❷ Add Cheddar cheese to the ground sirloin and re-secure the Processing Bowl's top. Pulse 3-5 times to chop and combine the cheese into the meat, leaving about ¼ inch chunks of cheese throughout.

❸ Carefully remove blades from Processing Bowl, and then scoop out the ground sirloin and cheese, one handful at a time. Use your palms to form into patties. Makes 4 quarter pound patties.

❹ Grill, pan fry or broil burgers as you normally would. Some cheese will almost certainly explode out of these burgers as you cook; making thicker, rather than wider patties is recommended to keep the most intact. If pan frying or broiling, thick burgers will take around 5-6 minutes to cook well on each side. Be sure to scrape any cheese from the pan into the bun with the burger!

❺ Serve on large hamburger buns, topped with your favorite fixings.

 This can be done with any cheese, though I prefer a medium Cheddar cheese. Sharper Cheddar cheese does not melt up as gooey. Try with Swiss or even bleu cheese! Or try mixing cheese right into your next meatloaf!

Salmon **Burgers**

Throw these salmon burgers on the grill along with some lobster tails and jumbo shrimp for a seafood barbecue you won't soon forget. For chunkier salmon burgers, be sure to save a fillet to add in for the final 2 or 3 pulses.

Directions

❶ Place salmon fillets, onion, tartar sauce, lemon juice, breadcrumbs, salt and pepper in Master Prep™ Pro Processing Bowl. Secure Processing Bowl's top and pulse for about 10 seconds, until salmon is well ground and onions are well minced.

❷ Carefully remove blades from Processing Bowl, and then scoop out the ground salmon, one handful at a time. Use your palms to form into patties. Makes 4 quarter pound patties.

❸ Grill, pan fry or broil burgers as you would a hamburger. Grilling or pan frying ½ inch thick patties should take about 5 minutes on each side.

❹ Serve topped with additional tartar sauce on a hamburger bun or wheat toast with lettuce and tomato or your favorite fixings.

This recipe also makes a great salmon cake appetizer for a party or get together, in place of the more typical crab cakes. Simply triple the amount of breadcrumbs added and form into small, 2 inch round cakes. Bake on a sheet pan at 400 degrees for 12-15 minutes.

Shopping **List**

1 pound raw salmon fillets, boneless and skinless

½ onion, peeled and sliced in half again

¼ cup tartar sauce

2 teaspoons lemon juice

2 tablespoons breadcrumbs

½ teaspoon salt

¼ teaspoon fresh black pepper

hamburger buns and fixings, optional

Serves **4**

Pro Processing **Bowl**

Really **Veggie Burgers**

A good recipe for a veggie burger may be a necessity in any vegetarian's repertoire of dishes, but done right, it can also be a real treat for non-vegetarians as well. I do like to prepare my Homemade Veggie Burgers whenever I also prepare traditional beef burgers to offer everyone a meat free alternative, or simply an alternative at all.

Shopping **List**

1 can (15 ounces) garbanzo beans, drained

1 large egg

¼ of 1 onion, peeled

½ cup fresh spinach

½ cup mushrooms

⅓ cup panko breadcrumbs

1 tablespoon all purpose flour

2 teaspoons vegetable oil

½ packet powdered ranch salad dressing mix

wheat buns and fixings, optional

Serves **4**

Directions

1 Place garbanzo beans, egg, onion, spinach, mushrooms, breadcrumbs, flour, vegetable oil and ranch salad dressing mix in Master Prep™ Pro Processing Bowl. Secure Processing Bowl's top and pulse for about 10 seconds, until garbanzo beans are mashed and onions are well minced.

2 Carefully remove blades from Processing Bowl, and then scoop out the mixture, one handful at a time. Use your palms to form into patties. Makes 4 patties.

3 Pan fry burgers over medium high heat in a nonstick pan greased with vegetable oil or a good amount of nonstick cooking spray. Fry until lightly browned, about 5 minutes on each side.

4 Serve on a wheat bun with your favorite fixings.

 For even crispier veggie burgers, dip the patties in additional panko breadcrumbs before pan frying. ¼ cup of drained, canned black beans can be added to the mixture right before forming the patties for a little bit more texture.

Turkey **Burgers**

These turkey burgers have more than a few secret ingredients. When you're working with turkey, you can always use a little more flavor and the soy sauce in this recipe gives the burgers a slightly "beefier" taste.

Directions

❶ Place turkey breast, onion, garlic, breadcrumbs, soy sauce, ketchup, parsley flakes and pepper in Master Prep™ Pro Processing Bowl. Secure Processing Bowl's top and pulse for about 15-20 seconds, until turkey is well ground.

Shopping **List**

1 pound uncooked turkey breast, cut into 1 inch pieces
¼ of 1 onion, peeled
2 cloves garlic, peeled
2 tablespoons panko breadcrumbs
1 tablespoon soy sauce
2 tablespoons ketchup
2 teaspoons parsley flakes
½ teaspoon ground black pepper
wheat buns and fixings, optional

Serves **4**

❷ Carefully remove blades from Processing Bowl, and then scoop out the ground turkey, one handful at a time. Use your palms to form into patties. Makes 4 quarter pound patties.

❸ Grill, pan fry or broil burgers as you would a hamburger. Grilling or pan frying ½ inch thick patties should take about 6 minutes on each side. Use a meat thermometer to be sure that the internal temperature reaches 165 degrees.

❹ Serve on wheat buns with lettuce and tomato or your favorite fixings.

Bob's Tips

Ground turkey breast tends to get dry, but these burgers are pretty moist. To make them even moister, try adding 1 small zucchini after step 1, pulsing about 8 times to finely chop it into the meat.

DINNERS AND SIDES

MAIN COURSES

Pistachio Crusted Tilapia 60

Italian Style Meatballs 61

Lasagna Style Penne Bake 63

Spinach Stuffed Pork Loin 64

Turkey Meatloaf with Sun-dried Tomatoes and Parmesan 65

Ninja Pizza 67

Almond Crusted Chicken 68

Pecan Crusted Salmon 69

Cracker Crumb Meatloaf 71

Ground Sirloin Stuffed Peppers 73

Swedish Meatballs 74

SIDES

Confetti Coleslaw 75

Roasted Garlic Smashed Cauliflower 76

Refried Kidney Beans 77

Really Creamed Corn 77

Southern Cornbread Muffins 79

Yukon Gold Mashed Potatoes 80

Twice Baked Sweet Potatoes 81

Potato Pancakes 82

Pro **Chopper**

Pistachio **Crusted Tilapia**

dinners/sides

Pistachios are quite possibly the most overlooked, but loved ingredients around. Crusting a fish in pistachios is even more overlooked and almost certainly guaranteed to be loved by all who are lucky enough to be invited over for dinner!

Directions

1 Preheat oven to 375 degrees. Spray a sheet pan with nonstick cooking spray.

2 Place pistachios and Italian seasoning in the Master Prep™ Pro Chopper. Secure Chopper's top and pulse 4-5 times until pistachios are minced small.

Shopping **List**

nonstick cooking spray
1 cup unsalted pistachios, shelled
2 teaspoons Italian seasoning
3 tablespoons Dijon mustard
2 teaspoons honey
½ teaspoon garlic powder
½ teaspoon salt
¼ teaspoon pepper
4 tilapia fillets

Serves **4**

3 In a separate bowl, use a spoon to combine Dijon mustard, honey, garlic powder, salt and pepper.

4 Spread an even coat of the mustard sauce on the top of the tilapia fillets. Sprinkle pistachio mixture across the top of mustard and lightly press into. Place crusted tilapia fillets on greased sheet pan and bake for 10-15 minutes, until fish is flaky and crust is crunchy.

5 Serve over rice or with your favorite sides.

When shopping for tilapia, I always keep an eye out for domestic tilapia, as it is usually far better quality than those raised elsewhere.

 Pro **Pitcher**

Italian **Style Meatballs**

Between bottled pasta sauce and frozen meatballs, spaghetti and meatballs has become a dish that is quick, but also often rather generic and mundane. Instead, why don't you try combining my Italian Style Meatballs with my No-Cook Pizza and Pasta Sauce, recipe page: 130, for something a little more distinctive and exciting?

Directions

❶ Place all ingredients in Master Prep™ Pro Pitcher. Secure top and pulse for 10-15 seconds, until meat is ground.

❷ Carefully remove blades from Pitcher, and then scoop out meatball mixture, one extremely rounded tablespoon at a time. Use your palms to form into perfectly round balls.

❸ Cook using your favorite method for cooking meatballs, or bake on a greased sheet pan in a 350 degree oven for about 25 minutes; until a meat thermometer registers the internal temperature has reached 160 degrees.

❹ Serve over pasta with marinara sauce or on hoagie rolls with sauce and provolone cheese.

Shopping **List**

1 pound beef round or shoulder roast, cut into 1 to 2 inch pieces
⅓ cup Parmesan Herb Bread-crumbs, recipe page: 136
⅓ cup milk
1 large egg
2 ounces Parmesan cheese
2 cloves garlic, peeled
1 tablespoon parsley flakes
½ teaspoon dry oregano
1 teaspoon salt
½ teaspoon ground black pepper

Serves **4**

 Bob's Tips

For even moister meatballs, simmer them in marinara sauce for 20-30 minutes until cooked through. If sauce reduces too much, add a little bit of water to thin it out (though, you have to love a hearty tomato sauce).

dinners/sides

Pro Processing **Bowl**

Lasagne **Style Penne Bake**

This incredibly simple casserole is reminiscent of lasagna or stuffed shells with nowhere near the same amount of work. All you have to do is boil some water for the penne, gather the necessary ingredients and let the Ninja™ Master Prep™ Professional do the rest!

Directions

1 Preheat oven to 375 degrees. Boil pasta according to the directions on box. Drain and return to pot.

2 Place ricotta, Parmesan cheese, 1 cup of the mozzarella cheese, egg, Italian seasoning, parsley flakes, salt and pepper in the Master Prep™ Pro Processing Bowl. Secure Processing Bowl's top and pulse 4-5 times until well combined.

Shopping **List**

12 ounces dry penne pasta
16 ounces part skim ricotta cheese
2 ounces Parmesan cheese
1 cup plus 1 cup mozzarella cheese
1 large egg
1 teaspoon Italian seasoning
1 teaspoon parsley flakes
½ teaspoon salt
¼ teaspoon ground black pepper
1 batch No-Cook Pizza and Pasta Sauce, recipe page: 130

Serves **6**

3 Add No-Cook Pizza and Pasta Sauce to the penne pasta and stir until pasta is evenly coated.

4 Transfer penne pasta in sauce to a deep 8x8 or 9x9 baking dish. Remove blades from Master Prep™ Pro Processing Bowl and pour cheese mixture over top of pasta, spreading it out evenly with a knife. Top with remaining 1 cup of mozzarella cheese.

5 Place dish in oven and bake for 20-25 minutes until cheese begins to brown around the edges. Let cool for 5 minutes before serving.

About 2 cups of any store bought tomato sauce can be used in place of my No-Cook Pizza and Pasta Sauce. Try adding a layer of thinly sliced zucchini and yellow squash between the cheese and pasta for a ratatouille twist.

Pro Processing **Bowl**

Spinach **Stuffed Pork Loin**

This recipe for a spinach and cheese stuffed pork loin is not only delicious, but quite a sight to be seen too!

Directions

❶ Preheat oven to 350 degrees. Grease a sheet pan with the tablespoon of olive oil.

❷ Place garlic cloves in the Master Prep™ Pro Processing Bowl. Secure Processing Bowl's top and pulse 4-5 times until garlic is minced.

❸ Add fresh spinach leaves, ricotta cheese, egg, Italian seasoning and pepper to the minced garlic and re-secure top. Pulse 2-3 times until all ingredients are combined and spinach is chopped, but not liquefied.

❹ Use a long knife to butterfly, or slice the pork loin lengthwise, about ½ inch up from the bottom of the loin. Slice until you are about ¾ of the way deep, then unfold the meat and use the palm of your hand to flatten down the thicker side. If too thick, slice into the thick side in the same manner as the first butterfly you performed.

❺ Spread spinach and ricotta mixture evenly across the flattened pork loin. Carefully roll the stuffed loin up like a pinwheel, making sure to push any filling back in as it may try to escape. Wrap loin in baking twine and tie off at least three times throughout the roast.

❻ Generously season rolled and tied pork loin with salt and pepper. Place on the greased baking sheet and bake for 40-50 minutes, until a meat thermometer registers 150 degrees. Let cool for 5 minutes before removing twine and slicing into ½ inch slices to serve.

Shopping **List**

1 tablespoon olive oil
2 cloves garlic, peeled
1 cup fresh spinach leaves
1 cup part skim ricotta cheese
1 large egg
1 teaspoon Italian seasoning
¼ teaspoon pepper
2 pounds boneless pork loin
salt and pepper

Serves **4**

You can also use this method to stuff pork loin with my Fresh Basil Pesto, recipe page: 128.

dinners /sides

Pro **Pitcher**

Turkey **Meatloaf** with **Sun-dried Tomatoes and Parmesan**

The problem with most ground turkey sold in stores is that it's actually not that good for you! To keep it moist, they usually mix in loads of fat that this recipe for Turkey Meatloaf with Sun-dried Tomatoes and Parmesan gets around by soaking the breadcrumbs in milk.

Directions

❶ Preheat oven to 350 degrees. Soak breadcrumbs in milk for 15 minutes before preparing meatloaf.

❷ Place garlic and Parmesan cheese (unless cheese is already grated) in Master Prep™ Pro Pitcher. Secure top and pulse 5-7 times in quick bursts until garlic is minced.

❸ Add cubed turkey breast, sun-dried tomatoes, egg, olive oil, salt, pepper and breadcrumbs and milk mixture to the Master Prep™ Pro Pitcher. Secure top and pulse for 8-10 seconds, until meat is ground.

❹ Carefully remove blades from Pitcher and then scoop meatloaf mixture into a loaf or bread pan. Combine ketchup and Dijon mustard to make a topping and spread over top.

❺ Bake 50-60 minutes, or until internal temperature of meatloaf reaches 160 degrees. Let cool for 5 minutes before slicing.

Shopping List

¼ cup Parmesan Herb Bread-crumbs, recipe page: 136
¼ cup milk
2 cloves garlic, peeled
2 ounces Parmesan cheese
1 ½ pounds uncooked turkey breast, cut into 1 inch pieces
½ cup sun-dried tomatoes
1 large egg
1 tablespoon olive oil
½ teaspoon salt
¼ teaspoon ground black pepper
2 tablespoons ketchup
1 tablespoon Dijon mustard

Serves **4**

dinners/sides

Bob's Tips

Store bought breadcrumbs will work fine in this recipe, but I'd suggest buying seasoned breadcrumbs for the most flavor. They should still be soaked in milk to keep the turkey meat moist.

Pro **Chopper**

Ninja **Pizza**

Why would you ever cook frozen when making your own pizza at home can be this easy? The Ninja™ Master Prep™ Professional makes blending up your own pizza sauce and chopping fresh toppings a breeze. This Supreme style combo of toppings is merely a suggestion, so feel free to chop up a few of your favorites as well!

Directions

1 Preheat oven to 450 degrees. Pre-bake crust, directly on the oven rack, for 5 minutes. Transfer to a sheet pan.

2 Top crust with pizza sauce and then ¾ of the mozzarella cheese.

3 Place onion in Master Prep™ Pro Chopper and pulse in 3-5 short pulses, just until chopped. Arrange over top of pizza. Repeat with black olives and then green bell pepper, pulsing each in Pro Chopper 4-6 short pulses before arranging on pizza.

4 Top pizza with pepperoni slices. Cover all with the remaining ¼ of mozzarella cheese and sprinkle with Parmesan cheese.

5 Bake pizza on sheet pan 10-12 minutes, or until cheese is hot and bubbly. Let cool 3-5 minutes before cutting.

Shopping **List**

1 ready to top pizza crust (such as Boboli brand)

1 ½ cups No-Cook Pizza and Pasta Sauce, recipe page: 130

1 ½ cups mozzarella cheese

¼ of 1 red onion, peeled

½ cup black olives

½ of 1 small green bell pepper

15-20 slices pepperoni

2 tablespoons Parmesan cheese

Serves **4**

dinners/sides

Bob's Tips

Pre-baking the crust for the 5 minutes is not entirely necessary, but does give it just the right amount of crispiness. I find that baking the fully topped pizza directly on the rack for the full amount of time makes it too crunchy and too awkward to safely remove from the oven!

Pro **Chopper**

Almond **Crusted Chicken**

This recipe is for a chicken dish that uses a distinctive almond based coating that is a terrific alternative to plain breadcrumbs for adding a little texture and a lot of flavor. Even better, with only a small amount of regular breadcrumbs used, they're lower in carbohydrates than typical breaded chicken.

Shopping **List**

nonstick cooking spray
¾ cup raw almonds
¼ cup breadcrumbs
2 cloves garlic, peeled
½ teaspoon paprika
¼ teaspoon onion powder
½ teaspoon salt
¼ teaspoon ground black pepper
4 thin chicken breasts
1 large egg white

Serves **4**

Directions

❶ Preheat oven to 400 degrees. Spray a sheet pan with nonstick cooking spray.

❷ Place almonds, breadcrumbs, garlic cloves, paprika, onion powder, salt and pepper in the Master Prep™ Pro Chopper. Secure Chopper's top and pulse 15-20 seconds until almonds are a well grated, breadcrumb consistency.

❸ Transfer almond mixture to a plastic storage bag or large mixing bowl. Dip raw chicken breasts in egg white and then add to almond mixture, pressing them into the almonds on all sides to thoroughly coat.

❹ Lay coated chicken breasts flat on the greased sheet pan and bake for 20-25 minutes until internal temperature reaches 165 degrees.

❺ Serve over rice or with your favorite sides.

Bob's Tips

To make a Dijon sauce to top chicken: sauté 2 tablespoons butter, ¼ cup Dijon mustard, ⅓ cup dry white wine, 1 tablespoon lemon juice, 2 diced green onions, 1 teaspoon sugar and ½ teaspoon salt until hot.

dinners/sides

Pro **Chopper**

Pecan **Crusted Salmon**

Who ever said that salmon had to always be served grilled? I find this to be a great recipe if you would like to enjoy the appetizing taste and remarkable health benefits that salmon has to offer, but want it to be exciting as well!

Shopping **List**

nonstick cooking spray

½ cup pecans

1 ½ tablespoons honey

2 tablespoons Dijon mustard

1 tablespoon water

½ teaspoon salt

4 boneless, skinless salmon filets (about 6 ounces each)

Serves **4**

Directions

❶ Preheat oven to 375 degrees. Spray a sheet pan with nonstick cooking spray.

❷ Place pecans, honey, Dijon mustard, water and salt in the Master Prep™ Pro Chopper. Secure Chopper's top and pulse 5-7 times until pecans are minced small.

❸ Spread an even coat of the pecan mixture across the top of each salmon filet. Place crusted salmon fillets on greased sheet pan and bake for about 15 minutes.

❹ Serve over rice or with your favorite sides.

For a Maple Pecan Salmon, substitute 2 tablespoons of pure maple syrup in place of the honey in this recipe. If Dijon mustard isn't your thing, try 2 tablespoons of low sodium soy sauce for a sweet and salty Asian flair.

dinners/sides

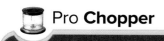

Pro **Chopper**

Cracker **Crumb Meatloaf**

Who doesn't love the flavorful and delicious home cooking classic that is meatloaf? This recipe gives you everything the good ole' original has to offer, but with a little added crunch from buttery crackers.

Directions

❶ Preheat oven to 350 degrees.

❷ Place crackers, onion, egg, half and half, garlic powder, parsley, Parmesan cheese, salt and pepper in Master Prep™ Pro Chopper. Secure top and pulse for 7-10 short pulses, until onion is finely chopped.

❸ In a large mixing bowl, combine onion mixture and ground beef and then scoop the meatloaf mixture into a loaf or bread pan.

Shopping **List**

8 buttery crackers (such as Ritz)
¼ of 1 onion, peeled
1 large egg
¼ cup half and half
½ teaspoon garlic powder
¼ cup fresh parsley
¼ cup Parmesan cheese
1 teaspoon salt
¼ teaspoon ground black pepper
1 ½ pounds ground beef
⅓ cup ketchup
2 tablespoons light brown sugar
additional crackers to top

Serves **6**

dinners/sides

❹ Combine ketchup and light brown sugar to make a topping and spread over top of loaf.

❺ Bake for 60-70 minutes, or until internal temperature of meatloaf reaches 160 degrees. Let cool for 5 minutes before slicing. Crumble additional crackers over top of ketchup layer before serving.

Bob's Tips

You can also make your own ground beef in the Ninja™ Master Prep™ Professional to start this recipe. Chunks of round or chuck roast work best, but you can even use inexpensive (and already chunked) stew meat.

 Pro Processing **Bowl**

Ground **Sirloin Stuffed Peppers**

With this recipe and the Ninja™ Master Prep™ Professional you can make the freshest ground steak to present in this unique and exciting way. Try making this dish with green, red, yellow or orange bell peppers, or one of each!

Directions

1 Preheat oven to 350 degrees. Cut tops off bell peppers and scrape out seeds and membranes.

2 Place sirloin steak and onion in the Master Prep™ Pro Processing Bowl. Secure Processing Bowl's top and pulse for 8-10 seconds, until sirloin is ground and onions are finely minced throughout.

Shopping **List**

4 bell peppers
1 pound sirloin steak
1 onion, peeled and quartered
1 cup crushed tomatoes (canned)
1 cup cooked rice
½ teaspoon allspice
1 teaspoon salt
½ teaspoon ground black pepper
½ cup Cheddar cheese, shredded

Serves **4**

3 Transfer sirloin mixture to a sauté pan over medium high heat. Sauté 5 minutes until sirloin begins to brown and fat cooks out.

4 Drain meat mixture and stir in remaining ingredients, except for the Cheddar cheese. Spoon the finished meat stuffing into the 4 hollowed out bell peppers. Top with a large pinch of Cheddar cheese.

5 Bake on a sheet pan, covered with aluminum foil, for about 40 minutes, until peppers are tender to the touch.

 Save the tops of the bell peppers in step 1 and bake them on the sheet pan alongside the stuffed peppers to place back on top for a beautiful serving presentation.

Swedish **Meatballs**

This recipe for Swedish Meatballs and its accompanying gravy offers a succulent and flavorful option for your next dinner. Consider trying them with my Yukon Gold Mashed Potatoes, recipe page: 80, for a slight twist on the classic Swedish meal of Swedish Meatballs and boiled potatoes.

Directions

❶ Preheat oven to 350 degrees. Soak white bread in milk for 15 minutes prior to making meatballs.

❷ Place white bread and milk, beef pieces, egg, parsley flakes, onion powder, nutmeg, allspice, salt and pepper in Master Prep™ Pro Processing Bowl. Secure top and pulse for 10-15 seconds, until meat is ground.

Shopping **List**

1 slice white bread
⅓ cup milk
1 pound beef round or shoulder roast, cut into 1 to 2 inch pieces
1 large egg
1 ½ tablespoons parsley flakes
½ teaspoon onion powder
⅛ teaspoon nutmeg
⅛ teaspoon allspice
1 teaspoon salt
½ teaspoon pepper
16 ounces sour cream
1 cup beef broth
¼ teaspoon white pepper

Serves **4**

❸ Carefully remove blades from Processing Bowl, and then scoop out meatball mixture, one extremely rounded tablespoon at a time. Use your palms to form into perfectly round balls.

❹ Bake on a greased sheet pan for about 25 minutes; until a meat thermometer registers the internal temperature has reached 160 degrees.

❺ While meatballs are baking, prepare the gravy by adding sour cream, beef broth and white pepper to a sauce pot over medium heat. Bring up to a simmer and cook for 5 minutes, stirring constantly.

❻ Serve meatballs alongside mashed potatoes, and smothered in gravy.

 Bob's Tips

For something different: I like Swedish Meatballs served alongside gnocchi (Italian potato dumplings) rather than mashed potatoes.

dinners /sides

Pro **Pitcher**

Confetti **Coleslaw**

When you've got the Ninja™ Master Prep™ Professional there is no need to buy pre-packaged coleslaw. Instead, start with a full head of cabbage and the following ingredients, and watch them turn into a delicious finely chopped coleslaw that you're sure to love!

Directions

❶ Place mayonnaise, buttermilk, milk, vinegar, sugar, onion powder, garlic powder, celery salt, and ground black pepper in a large mixing bowl and stir to make the dressing.

❷ Place baby carrots in Master Prep™ Pro Pitcher.

❸ Remove outermost leaves from cabbage and discard. Cut head of cabbage into eighths and place into Master Prep™ Pro Pitcher. Secure Pitcher's top and pulse 5-7 quick times until cabbage and carrots are finely chopped. (Depending on the size of cabbage, you may need to pulse in two batches.)

❹ Transfer chopped cabbage and carrots to the large mixing bowl with dressing mixture. Mix well to combine.

❺ Refrigerate for 1 hour to let the flavors mingle before serving.

Shopping **List**

1 cup mayonnaise
½ cup buttermilk
¼ cup milk
2 tablespoons vinegar
⅓ cup sugar
½ teaspoon onion powder
½ teaspoon garlic powder
1 teaspoon celery salt
½ teaspoon ground black pepper
1 head cabbage
6 baby carrots

Serves **12**

dinners/sides

Bob's Tips

To make an Apple Walnut Coleslaw: substitute cider vinegar in place of the white vinegar and add 1 peeled and cored apple to the Master Prep™ Pro Pitcher in step 2. Pulse ½ cup of walnuts separately in the Master Prep™ Pro Pitcher, just 2-3 times until chopped. Sprinkle chopped walnuts over slaw just before serving.

Pro **Pitcher**

Roasted **Garlic Smashed Cauliflower**

Although this recipe creates a healthy and appetizing side dish in its own right, many find that mashed cauliflower makes a great alternative to mashed potatoes. Cauliflower certainly provides certain benefits that you won't find in your average potato, such as high levels of vitamin C and fiber, but low levels of carbohydrates.

Shopping **List**

1 small head cauliflower

6 cloves roasted garlic, peeled (see tips)

2 ounces Parmesan cheese

3 tablespoons butter, softened

2 teaspoons parsley flakes

salt and pepper to taste

Serves **4**

Directions

1 Chop cauliflower into large florets, only disposing of the toughest stalks; boil for 6 minutes, until very soft.

2 Drain cauliflower extremely well and place in Master Prep™ Pro Pitcher while still hot. Add remaining ingredients and secure the Pitcher's top.

3 Pulse for 10-15 seconds, until cauliflower is creamy and nearly smooth.

4 Salt and pepper to taste and serve immediately. If the smash has cooled, transfer to a microwave safe dish and microwave for 1 minute to reheat.

To roast garlic: preheat the oven to 400 degrees and line a baking sheet with foil. Lay garlic cloves out in a single layer and cover with another sheet of aluminum foil. Bake for 15-20 minutes until cloves turn a golden brown. The peel is always easier to remove after roasting.

dinners/sides

 Pro Processing **Bowl**

Refried **Kidney Beans**

There are simply some occasions and some meals that call for a pairing of refried beans. If you're tired of the normal pinto bean based refried beans that you usually find, I think you'll love this recipe that calls for red kidney beans instead.

❶ Place all ingredients in the Master Prep™ Pro Processing Bowl. Secure the top and pulse 5-7 times until combined, but chunky.

❷ Carefully remove blades from Master Prep™ Pro Processing Bowl and microwave for 2 minutes, stirring halfway through. Serve hot.

Shopping **List**

2 cans (14 ounces) red kidney beans, drained and rinsed

2 tablespoons vegetable oil

1 small onion, peeled and quartered

1 tomato, top trimmed off and quartered

½ teaspoon cumin

¼ teaspoon coriander

1 teaspoon salt

Serves **6**

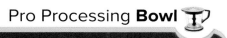 Pro Processing **Bowl**

Really **Creamed Corn**

It's hard to find someone that doesn't love creamed corn. Surprisingly, few people have actually made a batch from scratch, even though it's delicious!

❶ Place half of the corn kernels in the Master Prep™ Pro Processing Bowl. Pulse for 10 seconds, until pureed.

❷ Heat butter, pureed corn, and remaining whole corn kernels in a sauce pan over medium high heat, until sizzling.

1 bag (20 ounces) frozen corn kernels, thawed

2 tablespoons butter

½ cup heavy whipping cream

¼ cup milk

¼ teaspoon vanilla extract

1 ½ tablespoons sugar

½ teaspoon salt

Serves **4**

❸ Stirring constantly, add in remaining ingredients. Reduce heat to low and simmer 2 minutes. Serve hot.

 Pro **Pitcher**

Southern **Cornbread Muffins**

What do barbecues, a homestyle turkey dinner, and a bean soup such as my Cuban Black Bean Soup, recipe page: 48, have in common? They all go perfectly with a nice hot batch of cornbread muffins!

Directions

1 Preheat oven to 350 degrees. Spray a 12 cup muffin pan with nonstick cooking spray.

2 Place all ingredients in the Master Prep™ Pro Pitcher. Secure Pitcher's top and pulse for 8-10 seconds, until well mixed and free of lumps.

3 Fill greased muffin cups with equal amounts of batter and bake for 15-20 minutes, until a toothpick inserted into the center comes out clean. Let cool for 5 minutes before serving.

Shopping **List**

nonstick cooking spray

1 cup all purpose flour

1 cup cornmeal

1 large egg

1 cup milk

4 tablespoons butter, softened

3 teaspoons baking powder

⅓ cup sugar

1 teaspoon salt

Serves **12**

dinners/sides

 Bob's Tips

To make corn filled corn muffins, cut the milk down to ½ of a cup and add 1 can (14 ounces) of creamed corn. Or try cheesy corn muffins by adding a large pinch of shredded Cheddar cheese to the top of each muffin in the muffin pan before baking.

Pro **Pitcher**

Yukon Gold Mashed Potatoes

Yukon Gold potatoes, with their higher water and lower starch content than the Russet potato, in my opinion, make the creamiest mashed potatoes possible. They also come with the added bonus of not needing to be peeled!

Directions

❶ Boil cubed potatoes for 8-10 minutes, until tender.

❷ Drain potatoes extremely well and place in Master Prep™ Pro Pitcher while still hot. Add remaining ingredients and secure the Pitcher's top.

Shopping List

6 Yukon gold potatoes, cubed, skin on

2 cloves garlic, peeled

¼ cup sour cream

3 tablespoons milk

½ teaspoon onion powder

¼ cup fresh parsley leaves

salt and pepper to taste

Serves **6**

❸ Pulse only 3-4 times, removing top to check their consistency. Over processing will disintegrate their starch and make them very sticky. Re-secure top and pulse until your desired consistency has been reached, only pulsing in quick bursts and stopping to check for texture each time.

❹ Salt and pepper to taste and serve with butter, sour cream and chives, or gravy. If potatoes have cooled, transfer to a microwave safe dish and microwave for 1-2 minutes, until hot.

Bob's Tips

Whether you are using the Ninja™ Master Prep™ Professional or not; here are two great ways to salvage the gluey consistency of over-mashed, mashed potatoes. 1. Boil an extra potato worth of potato cubes and reserve to mash in if things go wrong. 2. Stir in boxed potato flakes a tablespoon at a time until the starchiness returns.

Pro Processing **Bowl**

Twice **Baked Sweet Potatoes**

These Twice Baked Sweet Potatoes are a holiday hit that are so good; you'll definitely want to bake them—twice—all year round.

Directions

❶ Preheat oven to 400 degrees, line a sheet pan with aluminum foil and bake sweet potatoes on the second to lowest rack for about 50 minutes, or until fork tender. Let potatoes cool for 10 minutes.

❷ Slice potatoes in half lengthwise and scoop out flesh, transferring it into the Master Prep™ Pro Processing Bowl. Leave just about ⅓ of an inch of flesh behind in the potato skin so that skins stay somewhat sturdy.

❸ Add heavy cream, milk, butter, maple syrup, cinnamon and salt to the potatoes in the Master Prep™ Pro Processing Bowl. Secure Processing Bowl's top and pulse for 10 seconds, until all ingredients are combined and smooth.

❹ Carefully remove blades from Processing Bowl and use a large spoon to spoon equal amounts of the pureed potato back into the potato skins.

❺ Place pecans and brown sugar in the Master Prep™ Pro Chopper. Secure top and pulse 3-5 times, until pecans are chopped. Sprinkle mixture over top of the potatoes. Bake potatoes for an additional 10 minutes until filling hardens slightly. Serve hot.

Shopping **List**

4 sweet potatoes, skin on
¼ cup heavy cream
¼ cup milk
3 tablespoons butter
1 tablespoon maple syrup
½ teaspoon cinnamon
¼ teaspoon salt
½ cup pecans
1 tablespoon light brown sugar

Serves **4**

For the best looking Twice Baked Potatoes, pipe the filling back into the potato skins using a pastry bag and pastry tip.

dinners/sides

Potato **Pancakes**

This recipe for potato pancakes, or latkes, is an interesting change from the ordinary potato side dishes. Kids love them too—as they're essentially a cross between two foods children find irresistible—pancakes and tater tots!

Directions

❶ Place all ingredients in the Master Prep™ Pro Processing Bowl. Secure Processing Bowl's top and pulse for 5-10 seconds, until all ingredients are finely minced and clumping together.

❷ Heat oil in a large sauté pan over medium high heat. Spoon rounded tablespoons of the potato pancake batter into pan and fry 2-3 minutes on each side, until golden brown. Repeat until batter is depleted.

❸ Salt to taste while still hot and serve hot or cold.

Shopping **List**

3 large potatoes, peeled and quartered

¼ of 1 onion, peeled

1 large egg

1 teaspoon lemon juice

2 tablespoons all purpose flour

¼ teaspoon baking powder

2 teaspoons parsley flakes

¼ teaspoon pepper

3 tablespoons vegetable oil

salt to taste

Serves **4**

Bob's Tips

Traditionally, potato pancakes are often served with apple sauce, which you can also prepare in the Ninja™ Master Prep™ Professional by following the recipe on page: 132.

dinners/sides

FROZEN **DRINKS**

FROZEN SPECIALTIES

Fresh Watermelon Slush 85
Mocha Cappuccino 86
Apple Carrot Blast 86
Frozen Lemonade 87
Pineapple Breeze 87
Cranberry Twist 88
"White" Mango Ice 89
Ninja Snow Cones 90
Vanilla Coffee Ice 91
Orange and Cream 93
Key Lime Pie Ice 94
Chocolate Raspberry Rumble 95

FROZEN COCKTAILS

The Best Frozen Margarita 96
Creamy Piña Colada 97
Strawberry Daiquiri 98
Peach Daiquiri 98
Mudslide 99
Strawberry Mango Colada 101
Spiked Fruit Punch 102

 Pro **Pitcher**

Fresh **Watermelon Slush**

This Fresh Watermelon Slush is so thick and refreshing that I'm not quite sure I should call it a frozen drink at all. On a hot summer day, I'd call it dessert! This recipe is one of the simplest around, which is a good thing because you won't want to be following too many directions in time that would be better spent relaxing with a glass of Fresh Watermelon Slush!

Shopping **List**

4 cups watermelon, seeded and cubed

1 cup lemon lime soda

Serves **3**

Directions

1 Place cubed watermelon into freezer for at least 2 hours, until frozen solid.

2 Place frozen watermelon cubes in the Master Prep™ Pro Pitcher and then add lemon lime soda over top. Secure the top and pulse for 10-20 seconds, until smooth and creamy.

3 Serve garnished with a wedge of fresh watermelon or lime.

 Depending on how ripe the watermelon is, you may want to add a dash of sugar or sugar substitute to sweeten things up. Add a kiwi and replace the lemon lime soda with white grape juice for a different drink altogether!

frozen drinks

Pro **Pitcher**

Mocha **Cappuccino**

I'm not naming brand names, but making this recipe for a Mocha Cappuccino frozen drink could save "Star" coffee fanatics something like five bucks a day!

❶ Fill one half of a 16 cube ice cube tray with espresso and the other half with 1 cup milk. Freeze for at least 3 hours, or until frozen solid.

Shopping **List**

1 cup espresso

1 cup, plus ½ cup milk

6 teaspoons sugar or 3 packets sugar substitute

2 tablespoons chocolate syrup

whipped cream, for garnish

Serves **2**

❷ Place espresso and milk cubes in the Master Prep™ Pro Pitcher and then add sugar, chocolate syrup and the remaining ½ cup of milk over top. Secure the top and pulse for 10-20 seconds, until smooth and creamy. Serve with whipped cream.

 Pro **Pitcher**

Apple **Carrot Blast**

This fruit and vegetable fusion is a real blast in a glass! Oh, and it's also pretty wholesome too. I just learned that the Japanese word for carrot is "ninjin" so it is clear that carrots and the Ninja™ Master Prep™ Professional are the perfect match. Or maybe I'm just delving too far into carrot facts.

1 cup carrot juice

1 cup, plus ½ cup apple juice

1 teaspoon lemon juice

Serves **2**

❶ Fill one half of a 16 cube ice cube tray with carrot juice and the other half with 1 cup of the apple juice. Freeze for at least 3 hours, or until frozen solid.

❷ Place carrot and apple juice cubes in the Master Prep™ Pro Pitcher and then the lemon juice and ½ cup of apple juice over top. Secure the Pitcher's top and pulse for 10-20 seconds, until smooth and creamy. Serve immediately.

frozen drinks

 Pro **Pitcher**

Frozen **Lemonade**

Frozen lemonade is a classic that I've been making for as long as I can remember. Now the Ninja™ Master Prep™ Professional is making them smoother and creamier than ever… just like the frozen lemonade I would get at the Fair years ago.

Shopping **List**

2 cups, plus ½ cup lemonade

1 teaspoon lemon zest

2 teaspoons sugar or 1 packet sugar substitute

Serves **2**

❶ Fill one 16 cube ice cube tray with lemonade. Freeze for at least 3 hours, or until frozen solid.

❷ Place lemonade cubes in the Master Prep™ Pro Pitcher and then add lemon zest and the remaining ½ cup of lemonade over top. Secure the Pitcher's top and pulse for 10-20 seconds, until smooth and creamy. Serve garnished with a lemon wedge.

Pro **Pitcher**

Pineapple **Breeze**

I can't think of many things that go together better than a hot summer day, the pool-side and a refreshing frozen treat, and not much completes a beautiful day by the pool like the tropical combination of pineapple and coconut found in this refreshing and wonderfully simple frozen beverage. Keep a steady supply of pineapple juice ice cubes on hand so that it never has to end.

2 cups pineapple juice

½ cup coconut milk

Serves **2**

❶ Fill one 16 cube ice cube tray with pineapple juice. Freeze for at least 3 hours, or until frozen solid.

❷ Place pineapple juice cubes in the Master Prep™ Pro Pitcher and then add coconut milk over top. Secure the Pitcher's top and pulse for 10-20 seconds, until smooth and creamy. Serve garnished with toasted coconut or a wedge of fresh pineapple.

frozen drinks

Cranberry **Twist**

I've always been a sucker for cranberry juice as there's something special about a beverage that is tart and yet surprisingly sweet and refreshing, and this frozen specialty is one of my favorite ways to enjoy it. With cranberry being such an unrelenting flavor, it is great to also try combining it with other flavors such as orange and raspberry as the cranberry will still shine through.

Shopping **List**

2 cups cranberry juice cocktail

½ cup white grape juice

juice of 1 lime

2 teaspoons sugar or 1 packet sugar substitute

Serves **2**

Directions

❶ Fill one 16 cube ice cube tray with cranberry juice. Freeze for at least 3 hours, or until frozen solid.

❷ Place cranberry juice cubes in the Master Prep™ Pro Pitcher and then add white grape juice, lime juice and sugar over top. Secure the Pitcher's top and pulse for 10-20 seconds, until smooth and creamy.

❸ Serve garnished with a wedge of lime.

A lime yields about 2 tablespoons of lime juice, if you would rather substitute bottled juice for this recipe. If using 100% cranberry juice instead of cranberry juice cocktail with sugar added, you may want to double or triple the sugar to offset the tartness.

 Pro **Pitcher**

"White" **Mango Ice**

Mango nectar is one of my favorite breakfast drinks, so it was only natural that I give it a whirl in the Ninja™ Master Prep™ Professional. The result was so creamy and delicious, you'd swear I pureed pure, fresh mango. White grape juice is the secret ingredient that gives this an extra boost of sweetness (and the strange name)!

Shopping List

2 cups mango nectar or juice

½ cup white grape juice

Serves **2**

Directions

1 Fill one 16 cube ice cube tray with mango nectar. Freeze for at least 3 hours, or until frozen solid.

2 Place mango cubes in the Master Prep™ Pro Pitcher and then white grape juice over top. Secure the Pitcher's top and pulse for 10-20 seconds, until smooth and creamy.

3 Serve garnished with fresh mango or a pineapple ring.

 Bob's Tips

Mango nectar is usually found in cartons in the Spanish food aisle. If you are having trouble locating it, many companies sell some kind of mango juice cocktail in the regular juice aisle and even in the refrigerated section near the orange juice.

Ninja **Snow Cones**

Snow cones are also known as snowballs for a reason, and The Ninja™ Master Prep™ Professional turns ice into snow like no machine I've ever seen. I often find myself showing off this truly impressive ability of the Ninja™ Master Prep™ Professional by whipping up a batch of almost perfect snow to the delight of my friends and guests. Just keep some syrups on hand and your demonstrations will not only be amazing to witness, but also incredibly delicious!

Shopping **List**

ice

flavored syrup or powdered drink mix

Serves **2**

Directions

1 To make snow in the Ninja™ Master Prep™ Professional, fill the Master Prep™ Pro Pitcher with ice, no more than two-thirds of the way up. There is no need to add any additional liquid.

2 Secure the Pitcher's top and pulse in short bursts for 10-20 seconds, or until ice is completely pulverized into a fine powder. Use an ice cream scoop to scoop into a glass or paper cone cup.

3 Top with store bought snow cone syrups. To make your own syrups: follow the directions on any packet of powdered drink mix using the correct ratio of mix and sugar, but only ⅓ of the water. Heat in a sauce pan over medium-low heat until it simmers and sugar has dissolved. Refrigerate the resulting syrup until cooled.

Snow cone syrups may not be sold in your local grocery store, but are almost always sold in Super discount stores. The variety of flavors is usually not as large as just making your own out of powdered drink mix.

 Pro **Pitcher**

Vanilla **Coffee Ice**

I love coffee, but a steaming cup of joe is the last thing I'm thinking of on a hot summer afternoon. Over a watered down cup of iced coffee, I thought of this recipe for frozen Vanilla Coffee Ice. When the ice cubes are made of coffee, there's no way to get watered down!

Directions

❶ Fill a 16 cube ice cube tray with coffee. Freeze for at least 3 hours, or until frozen solid.

❷ Place coffee cubes in the Master Prep™ Pro Pitcher and then add milk, sugar and vanilla extract over top. Secure the Pitcher's top and pulse for 10-20 seconds, until smooth and creamy.

❸ Serve garnished with whipped cream.

Shopping **List**

2 cups coffee

½ cup milk

2 tablespoons sugar or 3 packets sugar substitute

1 teaspoon vanilla extract

whipped cream, for garnish

Serves **2**

 I prefer natural vanilla extract over the imitation vanilla extract for the best flavor. You can also skip the vanilla extract and sugar in lieu of 2 tablespoons vanilla coffee syrup, usually sold in clear plastic bottles in the coffee aisle.

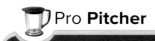 Pro **Pitcher**

Orange **and Cream**

This recipe is like one of those creamy ice cream filled frozen pops that I've loved since I was a kid. Replace the orange soda with grape soda and you've got a grape version of the frozen pop that is just as creamy and good. No need to chase down the ice cream truck for these!

Shopping **List**

1 cup vanilla yogurt

1 cup, plus ½ cup orange soda

whipped cream, for garnish

Serves **2**

Directions

❶ Fill one half of a 16 cube ice cube tray with vanilla yogurt and the other half with 1 cup of orange soda. Freeze for at least 3 hours, or until frozen solid.

❷ Place yogurt and orange soda cubes in the Master Prep™ Pro Pitcher and then add the remaining ½ cup of orange soda over top. Secure the Pitcher's top and pulse for 10-20 seconds, until smooth and creamy.

❸ Add sugar to taste, if desired. Serve garnished with whipped cream.

 In a pinch, milk and 1 teaspoon of vanilla extract can be substituted for the vanilla yogurt in this recipe. Orange juice can be substituted for the orange soda.

Key **Lime Pie Ice**

While the thought of key lime pie in a glass might not be mouth-watering at first, I assure you that my recipe for Key Lime Pie Ice is both delicious and refreshing! I'd say it's like key lime pie in a glass, but I'm pretty sure I just explained that that analogy is best unused here.

Shopping **List**

1 cup, plus ½ cup milk

1 cup limeade

½ teaspoon vanilla extract

4 teaspoons sugar or 2 packets sugar substitute

Serves **2**

Directions

1 Fill one half of a 16 cube ice cube tray with 1 cup milk and the other half of the tray with limeade. Freeze for at least 3 hours, or until frozen solid.

2 Place milk and limeade cubes in the Master Prep™ Pro Pitcher and then add the vanilla extract, sugar and the remaining ½ cup of milk over top. Secure the Pitcher's top and pulse for 10-20 seconds, until smooth and creamy.

3 Serve garnished with a lime wedge.

If the limeade you are using is sweet, but not very tart, add an additional tablespoon of lime or key lime juice to give the drink a little kick.

 Pro **Pitcher**

Chocolate **Raspberry Rumble**

Two for two, chocolate and raspberries have got to be two of my favorite things. With that in mind, a drink was not that far down the line. This sweetly embellished frozen drink is definitely one you'll want to save for dessert.

Directions

1 Fill a 16 cube ice cube tray with 1 and ½ cups of milk. Freeze for at least 3 hours, or until frozen solid.

2 Place milk cubes in the Master Prep™ Pro Pitcher and then chocolate syrup, sugar, raspberry preserves and the other ½ cup of milk over top. Secure the Pitcher's top and pulse for 10-20 seconds, until smooth and creamy.

3 Serve immediately garnished with fresh raspberries or shaved chocolate or both!

Shopping **List**

1 ½ cups, plus ½ cup milk

1 ½ tablespoons chocolate syrup

4 teaspoons sugar or 2 packets sugar substitute

2 tablespoons raspberry preserves

Serves **2**

frozen drinks

 Bob's Tips

This drink, or any of my frozen specialty drinks in this book, can be made lighter by substituting soy milk for the milk. Fat free milk also works well, but I actually find the soy milk to be thicker and more decadent!

Pro **Pitcher**

The Best Frozen **Margarita**

There has always been something delightfully exotic about a margarita that really takes me away from reality. So make a batch of margaritas and allow yourself to be taken away, worry free, because what's great about the Ninja™ Master Prep™ Professional is that you'll find you don't get any surprise large chunks of ice to ruin the illusion.

Shopping **List**

5 cups ice

1 can (6 ounces) frozen limeade concentrate

6 ounces tequila

2 ounces triple sec

Margarita salt, optional

Directions

Serves **4**

1 Fill Master Prep™ Pro Pitcher with ice to the 5 cup line.

2 Cover ice with limeade concentrate, tequila and triple sec. Secure the Pitcher's top and pulse for 10-20 seconds, until smooth and creamy.

3 Serve garnished with Margarita salt and a lime wedge.

To make Strawberry Margaritas: halve the limeade concentrate and substitute 3 cups of frozen strawberries for 3 cups of the ice.

 Pro **Pitcher**

Creamy **Piña Colada**

With its tropical flavors, the Piña Colada is the first cocktail that comes to my mind when I'm sitting pool-side or heading down to the beach. Luckily, the Ninja™ Master Prep™ Professional literally whips them up in a flash, so you won't be stuck inside making drinks on a beautiful summer day!

Shopping **List**

5 cups ice

8 ounces light rum

¾ cup coconut cream

1 cup canned crushed pineapple with juice

Serves **4**

Directions

❶ Fill Master Prep™ Pro Pitcher with ice to the 5 cup line.

❷ Cover ice with rum, coconut cream and pineapple. Secure the Pitcher's top and pulse for 10-20 seconds, until smooth and creamy.

❸ Serve garnished with fresh pineapple or maraschino cherries.

 Coconut cream is usually sold near the thinner coconut milk, but coconut milk will work in a pinch. For a smoother consistency, substitute pineapple juice for the crushed pineapple.

frozen drinks

Pro **Pitcher**

Strawberry Daiquiri

Hat do you get when you add a little rum and lime juice to a strawberry smoothie? A strawberry daiquiri of course, and what do I really need to say about the classic Strawberry Daiquiri other than it is a refreshing way to get a fun day started?

❶ Place ice, frozen strawberries, rum, lime juice and sugar in the Master Prep™ Pro Pitcher. Secure the Pitcher's top and pulse for 10-20 seconds, until smooth and creamy.

❷ Serve garnished with a fresh strawberry or a wedge of lime.

Shopping **List**

2 cups ice
3 cups frozen strawberries
8 ounces light rum
½ cup lime juice
⅓ cup sugar

Serves **4**

Pro **Pitcher**

Peach Daiquiri

ith a daiquiri's only real requirement being that their main ingredients be rum, lime juice and sugar, it is easy to imagine the numerous possible flavors of daiquiris. Personally, I have always enjoyed the almost syrupy sweetness of peaches as a main ingredient in a daiquiri.

2 cups ice
3 cups frozen peaches
4 ounces white rum
4 ounces peach schnapps
¼ cup lime juice
¼ cup sugar

Serves **4**

❶ Place ice, frozen peaches, white rum, peach schnapps, lime juice and sugar in the Master Prep™ Pro Pitcher. Secure the Pitcher's top and pulse for 10-20 seconds, until smooth and creamy.

❷ Serve garnished with a sprig of mint or fresh peach wedge.

frozen drinks

 Pro **Pitcher**

Mudslide

Pure decadence is the perfect way to describe this popular frozen cocktail that is truly more of a dessert than anything else. If you want to go all the way and erase any question as to its dessert status, you can substitute 2 scoops of ice cream for 2 cups of the ice. Adding in a banana is another delicious twist that I'm quite fond of.

Shopping List

5 cups ice

2 ounces vodka

3 ounces coffee liqueur

3 ounces Irish cream liqueur

2 tablespoons chocolate syrup

whipped cream

Serves **4**

Directions

1 Fill Master Prep™ Pro Pitcher with ice to the 5 cup line.

2 Cover ice with vodka, coffee liqueur, Irish cream liqueur and chocolate syrup. Secure the Pitcher's top and pulse for 10-20 seconds, until smooth and creamy.

3 Serve topped with whipped cream and a drizzle of chocolate syrup.

 Coffee liqueur may be a little pricey, especially with two other spirits to purchase. A double shot of chilled espresso may be substituted as long as you double the amount of Irish Cream liqueur.

 Pro **Pitcher**

Strawberry **Mango Colada**

This frozen cocktail isn't only a distinctive and refreshing alternative to the classic piña colada, but its layered presentation will be downright impressive at your next pool party. Luckily, with the Ninja™ Master Prep™ Professional it only looks like it takes a lot of work!

Directions

1 Place ice, rum, coconut cream and frozen strawberries in the Master Prep™ Pro Pitcher. Secure the Pitcher's top and pulse for 10-20 seconds, until smooth and creamy. Transfer mixture to a separate Pitcher or use a second Master Prep™ Pro Pitcher for the second half of the drink.

Shopping **List**

Strawberry Colada

1 cup ice

4 ounces light rum

¼ cup coconut cream

2 cups frozen strawberries

Mango Colada

1 cup ice

4 ounces light rum

¼ cup coconut cream

2 cups frozen mango chunks

Serves **4**

2 Place ice, rum, coconut cream and frozen mango in an empty Master Prep™ Pro Pitcher. Secure the Pitcher's top and pulse for 10-20 seconds, until smooth and creamy.

3 Layer the Strawberry and Mango Coladas in 1-2 inch layers, tapping the glass to settle before adding each layer on top of the other. Serve garnished with toasted coconut or fresh fruit.

Bob's Tips

To toast shredded coconut: preheat an oven to 350 degrees and spread coconut on a sheet pan in a thin layer. Bake 6-8 minutes, shaking sheet pan halfway through to stir around.

frozen drinks

Spiked **Fruit Punch**

The idea of spiked punch has always been to get the party started, and this recipe for a frozen Spiked Punch is sure to do just that. Just make sure that none of your house guests pull a fast one and spike this punch again—it's packing quite a punch as it is.

Shopping **List**

5 cups ice

1 can (6 ounces) frozen fruit punch concentrate

1 cup canned crushed pineapple with juice

juice of 1 lime

8 ounces vodka

Serves **4**

Directions

❶ Fill Master Prep™ Pro Pitcher with ice to the 5 cup line.

❷ Cover ice with fruit punch concentrate, crushed pineapple, lime juice and vodka. Secure the Pitcher's top and pulse for 10-20 seconds, until smooth and creamy.

❸ Serve garnished with a lime wedge or maraschino cherry.

 Try using flavored vodka to add yet another element to this fruity amalgamation. Strawberry, black cherry or orange flavored vodkas are all readily available and delicious in frozen cocktails.

frozen drinks

SMOOTHIES AND MILKSHAKES

SMOOTHIES

MILKSHAKES

 Pro **Pitcher**

Strawberry **Banana Smoothie**

Hands down, the basic Strawberry Banana Smoothie is one of the staples of smoothie recipes. No matter what wonderful, crazy and new recipes for smoothies that my Ninja™ Master Prep™ Professional allows me to try at home, I always find myself turning back to this classic smoothie that is, and always will be, perfection through simplicity.

Shopping **List**

3 cups frozen strawberries

2 ripe bananas, peeled

1 cup milk

2 tablespoons sugar or 3 packets sugar substitute

Serves **3**

Directions

❶ Place all ingredients in the Master Prep™ Pro Pitcher. Secure the top and pulse for about 45 seconds, until smooth and creamy. Drink should be completely smooth when you no longer hear pieces of frozen strawberry being chopped.

❷ Serve garnished with a fresh strawberry or slice of banana.

 Bob's Tips

Frozen strawberries sold in the frozen foods section of the grocery store are the easiest and most inexpensive way to make a smoothie, though they are not always the sweetest. Depending on your taste, you may want to add 2 teaspoons or 1 packet of sugar substitute to sweeten things up.

smoothies/shakes

Pro **Pitcher**

Berry **Mixed Up Smoothie**

There's not much more fundamental when it comes to smoothies than a classic berry smoothie, and what's better than being able to whip it up yourself when the mood strikes? This recipe is quick and easy, and can of course be tailored to fit your preferences; extra raspberries for me!

Shopping **List**

2 ½ **cups frozen strawberries**

½ **cup frozen blueberries**

½ **cup frozen raspberries**

1 **cup milk**

½ **teaspoon vanilla extract**

2 **tablespoons sugar or 3 packets sugar substitute**

Serves **3**

Directions

❶ Place all ingredients in the Master Prep™ Pro Pitcher. Secure the top and pulse for about 45 seconds, until smooth and creamy. Drink should be completely smooth when you no longer hear pieces of frozen berries being chopped.

❷ Serve garnished with whipped cream, fresh berries, or both!

 For a great breakfast smoothie, 1 ½ cups of fresh vanilla yogurt can be substituted for the milk, vanilla extract and sugar in this recipe. Or try a blueberry or raspberry yogurt for even more berry goodness!

 Pro **Pitcher**

Healthy **Fruit** and **Vegetable Smoothie**

This drink is fun, healthy and worth the time to assemble all the ingredients. You will never taste the spinach, but it adds a load of iron and color to this drink. I'm not a mathematician, but I'd say that this drink counts for just about all of your daily servings of fruit and vegetables!

Directions

❶ Place all ingredients in the Master Prep™ Pro Pitcher, ice cubes on top. Secure the top and pulse for about 60 seconds, until the entire drink is liquefied. Drink should be completely liquefied when you no longer hear pieces of ice being chopped.

❷ Serve garnished with fresh fruit.

Shopping **List**

1 cup pineapple juice

1 small carrot

1 cup cherry tomatoes

½ apple, unpeeled and cut in half again

1 kiwi, peeled

2 wedges watermelon, 2 inches each

1 wedge cantaloupe, 2 inches thick

6 strawberries

1 cup fresh spinach

1 slice ginger, ¼ inch thick

½ celery stalk

2 tablespoons sugar or 3 packets sugar substitute

6 ice cubes

Serves **4**

 The taste of this healthy smoothie is delicious when all of the ingredients are well combined, so be sure that you pulse it long enough to completely liquefy.

smoothies /shakes

Pro **Pitcher**

Tropical **Paradise Smoothie**

When you're in the mood for a delightfully tropical smoothie, there isn't a much better combination than the mango, kiwi and pineapple that is found in this recipe. If only I could think of a way to bring my Ninja™ Master Prep™ Professional down to the beach….

Shopping **List**

2 cups frozen mango

1 kiwi, peeled and quartered

½ cup pineapple juice

½ cup milk

1 ½ tablespoons sugar or 2 packets sugar substitute

Serves **2**

Directions

❶ Place all ingredients in the Master Prep™ Pro Pitcher. Secure the top and pulse for about 45 seconds, until smooth and creamy. Drink should be completely smooth when you no longer hear pieces of frozen mango being chopped.

❷ Serve garnished with a slice of fresh kiwi.

Try adding a scoop of low-fat vanilla ice cream or frozen yogurt to any smoothie for an even creamier drink. Replace the milk with coconut milk for something even more tropical!

smoothies/shakes

 Pro **Pitcher**

Protein **Packed Mocha Smoothie**

While the thought of drinking tofu can be off putting to some, trust me. This delightfully delicious smoothie provides you with a respectable dose of protein and iron without the unnecessary fat and calories that only good ole tofu can deliver. Let the Ninja™ Master Prep™ Professional surprise you with this smoothie that is both satisfying and energizing!

Shopping **List**

1 cup tofu, drained and cubed

1 cup vanilla yogurt

2 tablespoons chocolate syrup

1 ½ teaspoons instant coffee

1 ½ tablespoons sugar or 2 packets sugar substitute

8 ice cubes

Serves **2**

Directions

❶ Place all ingredients in the Master Prep™ Pro Pitcher, ice cubes on top. Secure the Pitcher's top and pulse for about 45 seconds, until smooth and creamy. Drink should be completely smooth when you no longer hear pieces of ice being chopped.

❷ Serve topped with a drizzle of chocolate syrup.

 Add a frozen banana for a thicker, creamier, Banana Mocha Smoothie. 2 scoops of a chocolate flavored protein powder and 4 extra ice cubes can be substituted in place of the tofu and chocolate syrup.

smoothies/shakes

Pro **Pitcher**

Mandarin **Orange Smoothie**

Other than being delicious, this recipe for a Mandarin Orange Smoothie also gets a nice boost from healthy, and wholesome, carrot juice. The orange color of carrot jucie blends so well into citrus drinks that it's an easy way to get kids to have their vegetables! I personally love the natural sweetness it adds.

Shopping **List**

2 cans (6 ounces each) mandarin orange segments, drained

1 cup ice

1 cup vanilla nonfat yogurt

½ cup orange juice

½ cup carrot juice

Serves **4**

Directions

❶ Place drained oranges into freezer for at least 2 hours, or until frozen solid.

❷ Place frozen oranges and ice in the Master Prep™ Pro Pitcher. Secure the Pitcher's top and pulse for 7-10 short pulses, or until snow.

❸ Add vanilla yogurt, orange juice, and carrot juice, re-secure the Pitcher's top and pulse for 5-7 long pulses, or until smooth and creamy.

❹ Serve garnished with a wedge of fresh orange.

Whenever I am buying canned fruit, I always look for the cans that pack the fruit in 100% juice, not heavy or light syrup. All of the extra sugar in the syrup is not only bad for you, but really takes away from the natural flavor of the fruit.

smoothies /shakes

Pro **Pitcher**

Green **Apple Goodness Smoothie**

The best part of making smoothies at home is that you are able to make yourself the combinations you always hoped you'd find at a smoothie shop. All of the fruits in this smoothie are bold and bright, and combined they come together to make something unique and delicious.

❶ Place all ingredients in the Master Prep™ Pro Pitcher, ice cubes on top. Secure the Pitcher's top and pulse for about 60 seconds, until smooth. Drink should be completely smooth when you no longer hear pieces of ice being chopped.

❷ Serve immediately, topped with a slice of unpeeled, green apple.

Shopping **List**

2 green apples, peeled and cored
1 kiwi, peeled
1 cup white grape juice
1 ½ tablespoons sugar or 2 packets sugar substitute
6 ice cubes

Serves **2**

Pro **Pitcher**

Honey **Sweet Peach Smoothie**

I'm a huge peach lover, so I created this smoothie to pack in as much unadulterated peach flavor as I could. Still, for an even more concentrated peachy flavor, I find nectarines to be the peachiest of the peach family. I just don't recommend trying to say that last sentence ten times fast!

2 cups frozen peach slices
1 cup peach yogurt
½ cup milk
1 tablespoon honey

Serves **2**

❶ Place frozen peach slices in the Master Prep™ Pro Pitcher and then cover with remaining ingredients. Secure the Pitcher's top and pulse for about 45 seconds, until smooth and creamy. Drink should be completely smooth when you no longer hear pieces of frozen peach being chopped.

❷ Serve garnished with a light sprinkling of cinnamon, if desired.

smoothies/shakes

Pro **Pitcher**

Peanut **Butter Banana Smoothie**

Between the peanut butter and soy milk found in this recipe, this smoothie is so packed full of protein that you can even enjoy it for breakfast, knowing you'll get a strong start to your day. This smoothie also tastes great with a little whey protein powder added in for that little extra boost of protein that's great after a good work out.

Shopping **List**

1 banana, peeled and frozen

1 cup vanilla yogurt

2 tablespoons creamy peanut butter

3 tablespoons chocolate syrup

½ cup soy milk

2 teaspoons sugar or 1 packet sugar substitute

4 ice cubes

Serves **2**

Directions

❶ Place all ingredients in the Master Prep™ Pro Pitcher, ice cubes on top. Secure the Pitcher's top and pulse for about 45 seconds, until smooth and creamy. Drink should be completely smooth when you no longer hear pieces of ice being chopped.

❷ Serve topped with a drizzle of chocolate syrup.

Regular milk can be substituted for soy milk in this recipe. As strange as it sounds, cashew butter also works well in place of the peanut butter.

smoothies/shakes

Pro **Pitcher**

CranRazz Smoothie

What can I say? When these three ingredients come together in a smoothie it is pure perfection. The raspberries sweeten up the cranberries, and then the yogurt comes in and rounds it all out. Feel free to add a little bit of sugar or sugar substitute if you prefer your smoothies on the sweeter side.

Shopping List

1 cup frozen raspberries

1 ½ cups vanilla frozen yogurt

1 ½ cups cranberry juice cocktail

Serves **2**

Directions

❶ Place all ingredients in the Master Prep™ Pro Pitcher. Secure the top and pulse for about 45 seconds, until smooth and creamy. Drink should be completely smooth when you no longer hear pieces of frozen raspberries being chopped.

❷ Serve garnished with a fresh raspberry.

Bob's Tips

Try substituting orange sherbert for the frozen yogurt in this recipe for a citrus twist on this great smoothie! For a fresher orange taste, skip the sherbert in lieu of a teaspoon of orange zest and save the meat of the orange for a garnish.

smoothies/shakes

Pro **Pitcher**

Chocolate **Malt**

Let this recipe for a chocolate malted milkshake bring you back to the days of the classic soda-fountains, malt shops and drugstores, yes drugstores. You may no longer be able to get a delicious malt at a certain popular chain drugstore anymore, but with the Ninja™ Master Prep™ Professional you can absolutely enjoy one quickly and easily at home.

Shopping **List**

2 cups chocolate ice cream (2 large scoops)

1 ½ cups milk

1 tablespoon chocolate syrup

2 tablespoons malted milk powder

2 ice cubes

Serves **2**

Directions

❶ Place all ingredients in the Master Prep™ Pro Pitcher, ice cubes on top. Secure the Pitcher's top and pulse for about 45 seconds, until smooth and creamy. Drink should be completely smooth when you no longer hear pieces of ice being chopped.

❷ Serve topped with whipped cream and a drizzle of chocolate syrup.

The added chocolate syrup in this recipe helps keeps the milkshake rich after diluting it with milk. The two ice cubes are ground smooth by the Ninja™ Master Prep™ Professional, but help keep the temperature of the entire milkshake low, slowing it from melting.

smoothies/shakes

 Pro **Pitcher**

Cookies **and Cream Milkshake**

The combination of cream filled chocolate cookies and ice cream is such an obviously delicious mixture that no one seems to be able to decide who thought of it first! But who really cares? All that matters is that this milkshake is a classic and delicious hit!

Directions

1 Place ice cream, milk, vanilla extract and ice cubes in the Master Prep™ Pro Pitcher, ice cubes on top. Secure the Pitcher's top and pulse for about 30 seconds, until ice cubes are almost entirely broken up.

2 Add in chocolate sandwich cookies and re-secure the Pitcher's top. Pulse for 15 more seconds until milkshake is speckled with cookie bits, but cookies are not entirely liquefied.

3 Serve topped with whipped cream and a whole chocolate sandwich cookie.

Shopping **List**

2 cups vanilla ice cream (2 large scoops)

1 ½ cups milk

½ teaspoon vanilla extract

2 ice cubes

6 cream filled chocolate sandwich cookies

Serves **2**

smoothies/shakes

 Bob's Tips

I'm pretty sure you know which brand of cookie I'm referring to here, but just in case, let me tell you a story-o about a boy named Or… nevermind.

Pro **Pitcher**

Candy **Apple Milkshake**

While you could probably just put a real candy apple in the Ninja™ Master Prep™ Professional with some ice cream and create a Candy Apple Milkshake that way; I think this recipe is so reminiscent of the real thing, why would you waste a perfectly good candy apple? Besides, who can wait for Fall when candy apples are most plentiful?

Shopping **List**

2 cups vanilla ice cream (2 large scoops)

1 cup milk

½ cup apple sauce

¼ teaspoon cinnamon

2 ice cubes

caramel sauce

Serves **2**

Directions

1 Place ice cream, milk, apple sauce, cinnamon and ice cubes in the Master Prep™ Pro Pitcher, ice cubes on top. Secure the Pitcher's top and pulse for about 45 seconds, until smooth and creamy. Drink should be completely smooth when you no longer hear pieces of ice being chopped.

2 Drizzle caramel sauce around the inside of the serving glasses before pouring the milkshake into them.

3 Serve topped with whipped cream drizzled with more caramel sauce.

Most grocery stores sell plastic squeeze bottles of caramel sauce near the sprinkles and other ice cream toppings. The squeeze bottles work best, as opposed to the glass jars which are usually far thicker caramel sauces, meant to be served hot.

smoothies/shakes

 Pro **Pitcher**

Chocolate **Covered Banana Milkshake**

There's something wonderfully decadent about the combination of chocolate and bananas… well, really that's true of chocolate and any fruit! If you are feeling particularly self-indulgent, try adding strawberries as well.

Shopping **List**

2 cups vanilla ice cream (2 large scoops)

1 ½ cups milk

2 tablespoons chocolate syrup

1 banana, peeled

2 ice cubes

Serves **2**

Directions

❶ Place all ingredients in the Master Prep™ Pro Pitcher, ice cubes on top. Secure the Pitcher's top and pulse for about 45 seconds, until smooth and creamy. Drink should be completely smooth when you no longer hear pieces of ice being chopped.

❷ Drizzle chocolate syrup around the inside of the serving glasses before pouring the milkshake into them.

❸ Serve topped with whipped cream and another drizzle of chocolate syrup.

 I prefer to make this with vanilla ice cream and lots of chocolate syrup, rather than using chocolate ice cream to start. To me, it just tastes more like an old fashioned, frozen, chocolate covered banana.

smoothies / shakes

 Pro **Pitcher**

Peaches **and Cream Milkshake**

I've always felt that a nice peach milkshake was the best of the fruit milkshakes as the peach flavor really holds its own against the calming influence of the ice cream. Just don't tell the other fruit milkshakes I told you that....

Directions

❶ Place ice cream, milk, vanilla extract, sugar and ice cubes in the Master Prep™ Pro Pitcher, ice cubes on top. Secure the Pitcher's top and pulse for about 30 seconds, until ice cubes are almost entirely broken up.

❷ Add in peach slices and re-secure the Pitcher's top. Pulse for 15 more seconds until peach slices are chopped into small pieces, but not entirely liquefied.

❸ Serve topped with whipped cream and a fresh peach wedge.

Shopping **List**

2 cups vanilla ice cream (2 large scoops)

1 ½ cups milk

1 teaspoon vanilla extract

2 teaspoons sugar or 1 packet sugar substitute

2 ice cubes

1 peach, pitted and sliced

Serves **2**

This recipe works well with nectarines or apricots too. You may even want to try it with more tropical fruits like pineapple, papaya or mango. Simply substitute 1 cup of any fruit in place of the peach.

smoothies/shakes

Orange **Dream Milkshake**

What's better than the pairing of oranges and cream? I have a feeling others may agree as this milkshake reminds me of the creamy shakes you can get in the mall at a popular orange drink stand named after Julius Caesar.

Directions

1 Place all ingredients in the Master Prep™ Pro Pitcher. Secure the Pitcher's top and pulse for about 45 seconds, until smooth and creamy.

2 Serve topped with whipped cream.

Shopping **List**

2 cups vanilla ice cream (2 large scoops)

1 cup milk

¾ cup frozen orange juice concentrate

1 teaspoon vanilla extract

2 teaspoons sugar or 1 packet sugar substitute

Serves **2**

Bob's Tips

For a less tart milkshake, the milk and orange juice concentrate can be replaced by 1 ½ cups regular orange juice. To truly replicate the shakes in the mall, you may want to pulse an additional 30 seconds until the shake is thinner and beginning to froth.

smoothies / shakes

 Pro **Pitcher**

Mint **Chocolate Chip Milkshake**

This is one of those recipes that makes me feel like I really made something from scratch… well as much as I can without making the ice cream myself (which I can on page: 175). I hear of many people making this milkshake by simply mixing up some mint chocolate ice cream with some milk, but it's nice to be able to customize the level of peppermint to your preferences, just start by following the amount in the recipe before getting too daring.

Shopping List

2 cups vanilla ice cream (2 large scoops)

1 ½ cups milk

½ teaspoon peppermint extract

2 teaspoons sugar

¼ cup dark or semisweet chocolate (chips or squares or about ½ of a regular sized chocolate bar)

chocolate syrup

Serves **2**

Directions

❶ Place ice cream, milk, peppermint extract, sugar and dark chocolate in the Master Prep™ Pro Pitcher, dark chocolate on top. Secure the Pitcher's top and pulse for about 30 seconds, until smooth and creamy but while small chocolate pieces are still intact.

❷ Drizzle chocolate syrup around the inside of the serving glasses before pouring the milkshake into them.

❸ Serve topped with whipped cream and another drizzle of chocolate syrup.

 Bob's Tips
Garnish with a fresh mint leaf for the perfect presentation. If you'd prefer, 3-4 drops of green food coloring can be added to achieve the color you would come to expect from something so minty.

smoothies /shakes

Shake **for Wendy**

This chocolate milkshake that you eat with a spoon may remind you of a certain, "frosted" fast food shake that is one of a kind! With the Ninja™ Master Prep™ Professional, you can now whip one up quicker than you can make it through the drive-thru. Plus, you are already home, so you won't have to worry about it melting in the car!

Shopping **List**

2 cups vanilla ice cream (2 large scoops)

¾ **cup milk**

3 **tablespoons powdered-chocolate milk mix**

2 ice cubes

Serves **2**

Directions

1 Place all ingredients in the Master Prep™ Pro Pitcher, ice cubes on top.
Secure the Pitcher's top and pulse for about 45 seconds, until smooth and creamy. Drink should be completely smooth when you no longer hear pieces of ice being chopped.

2 Serve with a spoon!

To get the true experience of the original, you'll probably want to bake up some salted French fries for dipping! Yes, dipping into the shake. The salty fries and sweet shake are just about the definition of a guilty pleasure.

smoothies/shakes

SAUCES, CONDIMENTS AND DRESSINGS

SAUCES

CONDIMENTS

DRESSINGS

Pro Processing **Bowl**

Homemade **Apple Sauce**

What do you do when you have a whole bag of apples and their skin is starting to wrinkle? Well, you make apple sauce, of course! Homemade apple sauce is one of those small pleasures in life that reaffirms that fresher is better.

Shopping List

4 large apples, peeled and cored

⅔ cup water

2 tablespoons sugar

1 tablespoon light brown sugar

⅛ teaspoon cinnamon, optional

Serves **6**

Directions

❶ Place apples, water, sugar and brown sugar in a covered pot and heat on stove over medium heat, stirring occasionally until simmering.

❷ Lower heat to medium low and let simmer for 10 minutes.

❸ Remove from heat and let cool, uncovered, for 15 minutes.

❹ Transfer apple mixture to Master Prep™ Pro Processing Bowl, add cinnamon and secure the top. Pulse in quick bursts for about 1 minute or until your desired consistency has been reached. Cover and refrigerate for 1-2 hours before serving.

Try making this with apple juice or cider in place of the water for a bigger, bolder apple taste. Throw a handful of fresh strawberries into the Processing Bowl in step 4 for great Strawberry Apple Sauce without the artificial flavors you'd find in the store-bought variety.

sauces

 Pro **Chopper**

Greek **Cucumber Sauce**

Tzatziki Sauce is a Greek staple served with Gyros or just about any heavily marinated meat. This creamy yogurt, cucumber and dill sauce also soothes and cools the palette alongside spicy food. Or just try taking some warm pita bread for a dip and you've got a party!

Shopping List

1 medium cucumber

2 cloves garlic, peeled

1 tablespoon lemon juice

1 tablespoon fresh dill

2 cups plain yogurt

salt and pepper to taste

Serves **6**

Directions

1 Peel cucumber, and then slice in half lengthwise. Spoon out the softer, seed filled portion in the center and discard. Quarter the peeled and cleaned cucumber halves to fit into the Master Prep™ Pro Chopper.

2 Place cucumber, garlic, lemon juice and dill in Master Prep™ Pro Chopper. Secure the top and pulse 8-10 times, until well blended and cucumber is almost completely grated.

3 Skim any liquid off the top of yogurt, and then add to cucumber mixture in Master Prep™ Pro Chopper. Re-secure the top and pulse for 10-15 seconds, until well combined. Salt and pepper to taste and then refrigerate for at least 2 hours before serving to let the flavors mingle.

 The thicker consistency of Greek yogurt works best for this sauce, so keep an eye out for it in the dairy section of your grocery store. Secretly, I like sour cream even better!

Pro **Chopper**

Fresh **Basil Pesto**

Pesto, an Italian basil and pine nut sauce, shares the origin of its name with pestles; small sticks used with a mortar to crush the flavors out of food by hand. Thankfully, with the Ninja™ Master Prep™ Professional you can give the mortar and pestle and your arm, a rest and whip together a delicious sauce in seconds. Sharper, well aged cheese such as a nice wedge of Parmigiano-Reggiano works best for that authentic Italian taste.

Shopping **List**

½ **cup Parmesan cheese**
3 **cloves garlic, peeled**
½ **cup extra virgin olive oil**
⅓ **cup pine nuts**
1 **cup fresh basil leaves, packed**
salt and pepper to taste

Serves **6**

Directions

❶ Place Parmesan cheese and garlic cloves in the Master Prep™ Pro Chopper.

❷ Secure top and process in one long, 30 second pulse until cheese is grated. (Skip this step if using store bought grated cheese.)

❸ Add remaining ingredients, then fresh basil leaves last and secure top.

❹ Use 8-10 short pulses until pesto is a coarse, paste-like consistency.

❺ Salt and pepper to taste. Serve over your favorite pasta, or use as a fresh pizza or bruschetta topping. Also great on chicken or salmon!

If the strong flavors of pine nuts aren't for you, try substituting walnuts, cashews or blanched almonds. I like the blanched almonds best as their outer hull has been removed and won't turn your pesto brown.

 Pro **Chopper**

 Raspberry **Coulis**

This simple raspberry dessert sauce goes great drizzled on… well, just about anything. Try it on Crêpes, recipe page: 31 or try it underneath a cool slice of Creamy Key Lime Pie, recipe page: 160.

Shopping List

3 tablespoons water

⅓ cup sugar

8 ounces fresh raspberries

Serves **8**

Directions

1 Place water and sugar in a small sauce pan over medium heat, stirring until sugar has dissolved. Remove from heat.

2 Add Raspberries to dissolved sugar and then pour entire mixture into the Master Prep™ Pro Chopper. Secure the top and pulse in quick bursts for about 45 seconds, until smooth.

3 Optional: Drain coulis through a cheesecloth to remove seeds. Serve chilled.

 For the best presentation, use a sauce or old condiment bottle to drizzle the coulis around the plate or over top of a dessert.

No-Cook **Pizza and Pasta Sauce**

Although this sauce truly is fantastic on pasta, I find that I make this more often as a part of family pizza night. Everyone loves being able to top their own personalized pizza, and going the extra step to make your own pizza sauce makes the whole experience feel all that more special.

❶ Place all ingredients in the Master Prep™ Pro Processing Bowl. Secure the top and pulse 5 times for a chunky sauce. Pulse a few times more for an entirely smooth sauce.

❷ Serve on homemade pizzas or pasta.

Shopping **List**

2 cans (14 ounces each) diced tomatoes, drained
1 can (4 ounces) tomato paste
2 tablespoons olive oil
2 tablespoons Parmesan cheese
2 cloves garlic, peeled
½ teaspoon oregano
4 fresh basil leaves
1 teaspoon sugar
½ teaspoon salt

Serves **4**

Pro Processing **Bowl**

Easy **Hollandaise Sauce**

Although there are few ingredients, hollandaise sauce is known to be a little tricky, so let the Ninja™ Master Prep™ Professional help you to prepare this classic Eggs Benedict sauce with ease.

3 large egg yolks
2 tablespoons lemon juice
⅛ teaspoon cayenne pepper
¼ teaspoon salt
½ cup butter, melted and hot

Serves **6**

❶ Place egg yolks, lemon juice, cayenne pepper and salt in Master Prep™ Pro Processing Bowl. Secure top and pulse for 5 seconds until combined.

❷ Open pour spout on top of Processing Bowl and pulse the mixture in 10 second bursts as you slowly drizzle in the butter in a thin, yarn-thick stream. Continue this process until all of the butter has been combined and sauce is thick and creamy. Serve immediately while still warm.

🏆 Pro Processing **Bowl**

Natural **Peanut Butter**

After seeing the raw power of the Ninja™ Master Prep™ Professional, I knew that homemade peanut butter would be an obvious addition to this book. If you've never made peanut butter yourself, the texture may still be a little different than what you'd expect, but it will be more purely delicious than you've ever had it.

Shopping **List**

3 cups roasted peanuts, unsalted and shelled
¼ cup vegetable oil
2 tablespoons sugar
½ teaspoon salt

Serves **10**

❶ Place all ingredients in the Master Prep™ Pro Processing Bowl. Secure the top and pulse in 5 second bursts for about 2 minutes, until smooth and creamy.

❷ Store refrigerated. Will keep for about 6 weeks.

Pro Processing **Bowl** 🏆

Fresh **Cucumber Relish**

It seems that everyone knows that relish comes from cucumbers except the makers of store bought relish! They're usually so sweet that you'd be hard pressed to ever taste their cucumber beginnings.

1 large cucumber, sliced thick
¼ of 1 small white onion
2 tablespoons cider vinegar
2 teaspoons sugar
½ teaspoon celery salt

Serves **4**

❶ Peel cucumber, and then slice in half lengthwise. Spoon out the softer, seed filled portion in the center and discard. Quarter the peeled and cleaned cucumber halves to fit into the Master Prep™ Pro Processing Bowl.

❷ Place cucumber and all other ingredients in the Master Prep™ Pro Processing Bowl. Secure the top and pulse in quick bursts for about 15 seconds, until cucumber and onion are diced well. Refrigerate for at least 2 hours before serving to let the flavors mingle.

sauces

 Pro **Pitcher**

Avocado **Mayonnaise**

This egg-free avocado mayonnaise will bring a great southwestern flair to an old fashioned turkey club or even as the base for your next chicken salad! I like to add a dash of cayenne pepper for a little spice or even a small drizzle of chili oil, when I have it on hand.

Shopping **List**

1 avocado, skinned and pitted

1 tablespoon lime juice

1 tablespoon fresh cilantro

½ teaspoon salt

¼ cup canola oil

Serves **8**

Directions

❶ Place avocado, lime juice, cilantro and salt in Master Prep™ Pro Pitcher. Secure top and pulse for 10 seconds until combined.

❷ Open pour spout on top of Pitcher and pulse the mixture in 10 second bursts as you slowly drizzle in the canola oil in a thin, yarn-thick stream. Continue this process until all of the canola oil has been combined and mayonnaise is dense and creamy.

❸ Cover and store refrigerated for up to one week.

 Set out all of your ingredients before cutting into the avocado to keep it from turning brown before you've had the chance to turn it into mayonnaise. The acidity of the lime juice will stop the process dead in its tracks.

Homemade **Mayonnaise**

Though I'll admit to keeping a jar of the store-bought stuff in my fridge for the quick sandwich, I've always started with homemade mayonnaise for a good potato or chicken salad. It's just richer, its flavor doesn't overpower like some shelf brands tend to do, and now it's just plain easy to make.

Shopping **List**

1 large egg
1 large egg yolk
1 tablespoon lemon juice
¼ teaspoon dry mustard
½ teaspoon salt
1 cup canola oil

Serves **12**

❶ Place egg, egg yolk, lemon juice, dry mustard and salt in Master Prep™ Pro Processing Bowl. Secure top and pulse for 10 seconds until combined.

❷ Open pour spout on top of Processing Bowl and pulse the mixture in short bursts as you slowly drizzle in the canola oil in a thin, yarn-thick stream. Continue this process until all of the canola oil has been combined and mayonnaise is dense and creamy.

Pro Processing **Bowl**

Chipotle **Mayonnaise**

Chipotle peppers add a great smokiness and a nice kick to ordinary mayonnaise, making it the perfect topper for all sorts of sandwiches, especially my Turkey Burgers, recipe page: 58.

1 batch Homemade Mayonnaise, recipe above
1 tablespoon lime juice
1 tablespoon chopped chipotle chilies in adobo sauce
1 spring fresh cilantro

Serves **12**

❶ Prepare the Homemade Mayonnaise recipe as written above, substituting lime juice in place of the lemon juice.

❷ Add chipotle chilies and fresh cilantro to the finished mayonnaise and pulse in 6-8 more short bursts until all is combined.

sauces

Pro **Chopper**

Scampi **Butter**

This scampi butter is the perfect topper for a hot and juicy steak. Or store a batch in your fridge or freezer and add a scoop or two to a pan for a lightning fast shrimp or chicken scampi. It's like the sauce just makes itself!

Directions

❶ Place onion, garlic, parsley, salt, pepper, lemon juice and Worcestershire sauce in Master Prep™ Pro Chopper. Secure top and pulse 5-7 times in quick bursts until the garlic and onion begin to break up.

Shopping **List**

¼ of 1 small red onion

2 cloves garlic, peeled

2 sprigs fresh parsley

1 teaspoon salt

¼ teaspoon ground black pepper

1 ½ tablespoons lemon juice

¼ teaspoon Worcestershire sauce

½ cup (1 stick) unsalted butter or margarine, slightly softened

Serves **8**

❷ Remove top and use a spoon to push mixture down, away from the walls of the Chopper.

❸ Add butter, re-secure top and pulse in quick bursts for 30-45 seconds, until all ingredients are well combined, but still slightly chunky. Serve immediately or cover and refrigerate.

Bob's Tips

For the perfect steak topping butter medallions, scoop the finished scampi butter into plastic wrap and then roll it up into a cylinder, twisting both ends. Refrigerate until firm and it's ready to unwrap and slice!

sauces

Pro **Pitcher**

Parmesan **Herb Breadcrumbs**

I always figured, why worry about whether the packaged breadcrumbs you buy at the store are the perfect consistency or flavor to perfectly complement your dish when you can make them easily yourself! Breadcrumbs that are a little coarser add a great crunch to baked chicken or a little texture to pasta dishes.

Shopping **List**

1 baguette, sliced thin (about 5 cups sliced)

1 teaspoon Italian seasoning

2 ounces Parmesan cheese

1 teaspoon garlic powder

1 teaspoon onion powder

1 teaspoon salt

½ teaspoon sugar

½ teaspoon pepper

Serves **8**

Directions

❶ Preheat oven to 425 degrees. Bake bread slices, single layer, on a sheet pan for 8-10 minutes until lightly browned and crunchy.

❷ Place baked bread slices and remaining ingredients in Master Prep™ Pro Pitcher. Secure the Pitcher's top and pulse for 10-15 seconds in quick bursts until your desired consistency has been reached.

A fine, almost powdery consistency will coat chicken and other meats better for sautéing or baking. A coarser, chunky consistency adds more texture to a dish, and is especially good for topping casseroles!

Creamy **Parmesan Dressing**

With classic Italian flavors, this Creamy Parmesan Dressing makes the perfect topper for my Chopped Salad, recipe page: 53.

❶ Place all ingredients in the Master Prep™ Pro Processing Bowl. Secure the top and pulse in quick bursts for 45 seconds, until smooth and frothy.

❷ Salt and pepper to taste before serving over your favorite salad.

Shopping **List**

½ cup olive oil
4 ounces Parmesan cheese
2 cloves garlic, peeled
3 tablespoons red wine vinegar
1 tablespoon mayonnaise
3 tablespoons sour cream
½ teaspoon Italian seasoning
3 fresh basil leaves
salt and pepper to taste

Serves **6**

Pro Processing **Bowl**

Classic **Caesar Dressing**

This surefire classic recipe for Caesar Salad Dressing has been in my repertoire for as long as I can remember.

❶ Place egg, lemon juice, garlic, anchovy fillets, Parmesan cheese, and Worcestershire sauce in Master Prep™ Pro Processing Bowl. Secure the top and pulse in quick bursts for about 30-45 seconds, until garlic and Parmesan cheese are well minced.

❷ Add mayonnaise and olive oil to mixture in Master Prep™ Pro Processing Bowl. Re-secure the top and pulse for 10-15 seconds, until all ingredients are well combined. Pepper to taste before serving.

1 large egg
1 ½ tablespoons lemon juice
2 cloves garlic, peeled
1 anchovy fillet or 1 teaspoon anchovy paste
2 ounces Parmesan cheese
½ teaspoon Worcestershire sauce
¾ cup mayonnaise
¼ cup olive oil
ground black pepper to taste

Serves **6**

sauces

Pro Processing **Bowl**

Chunky **Bleu Cheese Dressing**

For whatever reason, store-bought bleu cheese dressing has always seemed to be the most lacking in the entire salad dressing aisle. Make it homemade with real chunks of fresh bleu cheese and you can never go back. Make it in a minute with the Ninja™ Master Prep™ Professional and you don't have to!

Directions

❶ Reserve ½ of the bleu cheese crumbles for the last step. Place other half of crumbles in the Master Prep™ Pro Processing Bowl.

❷ Add remaining ingredients to the Master Prep™ Pro Processing Bowl. Secure the top and pulse in quick bursts for 30-45 seconds until well combined.

❸ Carefully remove blades and set aside. Stir in remaining bleu cheese crumbles with a long spoon. Salt and pepper to taste and serve chilled. Cover and refrigerate for up to 4 days.

Shopping **List**

4 ounces bleu cheese crumbles
½ cup buttermilk
½ cup sour cream
5 tablespoons mayonnaise
1 teaspoon Worcestershire sauce
1 tablespoon vinegar
½ teaspoon garlic powder
½ teaspoon onion powder
salt and pepper to taste

Serves **10**

Bob's Tips Worcestershire sauce is an old steak house secret ingredient for bleu cheese dressing, but it can be omitted for a whiter, simpler dressing.

Pro Processing **Bowl**

Raspberry **Vinaigrette**

This fresh Raspberry Vinaigrette is a sweet and savory diversion from the ordinary. For a simple and elegant start to any meal, simply drizzle over mixed field greens garnished with hearts of palm and pecans.

❶ Place all ingredients in the Master Prep™ Pro Processing Bowl. Secure the top and pulse in quick bursts for 45 seconds, until smooth and well combined.

❷ For best flavor, refrigerate for 2 hours before serving to let the flavors mingle.

Shopping **List**

1 cup fresh raspberries
½ cup canola oil
½ cup cider vinegar
⅓ cup sugar
1 tablespoon Dijon mustard
½ teaspoon Italian seasoning
¼ teaspoon salt
¼ teaspoon black pepper

Serves **8**

Pro Processing **Bowl**

Sesame **Peanut Dressing**

This salad dressing is anything but ordinary. If you're tired of the same old Ranch, day in and day out, then this is for you! For a quick Asian Chicken Salad, serve over Iceberg lettuce with grilled chicken, mandarin oranges and crunchy wonton noodles.

❶ Place all ingredients in the Master Prep™ Pro Processing Bowl. Secure the top and pulse in quick bursts for 45 seconds, until smooth and well combined.

⅓ cup peanut butter
½ cup mayonnaise
1 cup milk
¼ cup low sodium soy sauce
¼ cup light brown sugar
1 tablespoon vinegar
1 tablespoon sesame oil
2 green onion stalks
¼ cup roasted peanuts
salt and pepper to taste

Serves **10**

❷ Salt and pepper to taste. For best flavor, refrigerate for 2 hours before serving to let the flavors mingle.

sauces

DESSERTS

WHIPPED

CANDIES

BAKED

Pro Processing **Bowl**

Real **Whipped Cream**

With the Ninja™ Master Prep™ Professional being the perfect tool to make a wide array of smoothies and desserts, how could I not include a recipe for their perfect garnish? Go ahead and try it on just about any smoothie, milkshake or dessert in this entire book for a treat that is truly homemade!

Shopping **List**

1 ¼ **cups heavy cream**

2 **tablespoons sugar**

1 **teaspoon vanilla extract**

Serves **6**

Directions

1 Place all ingredients in the Master Prep™ Pro Processing Bowl. Secure the top and pulse in short pulses for 15-25 seconds, or until cream is whipped to the consistency you desire.

2 Serve immediately. If storing, refrigerate in the Master Prep™ Pro Processing Bowl with lid on. Whipped cream will deflate over the course of several hours, but stored in the Master Prep™ Pro Processing Bowl itself, re-whipping will be a snap!

desserts

For the perfect whipped cream, place the Master Prep™ Pro Processing Bowl with blades in place, in the refrigerator for 15 minutes before whipping. Cream just whips better when everything is nice and cool.

Pro Processing **Bowl**

Chocolate **Mousse**

I always wonder how many people realize how incredibly simple it is to literally whip up your own batch of chocolate mousse. But even if you are one of the lucky ones who has enjoyed your own homemade mousse, you don't know how easy it can be until you've tried it in the Ninja™ Master Prep™ Professional. So whip some up and enjoy it on its own, as a dip for some fresh berries, or with a little drizzling of Raspberry Coulis, recipe page 143.

Shopping List

1 ¼ cups heavy cream

3 tablespoons chocolate syrup

Serves **4**

Directions

1 Place heavy cream and chocolate syrup in the Master Prep™ Pro Processing Bowl. Secure the top and pulse in short pulses for 15-25 seconds, or until light and fluffy.

2 Serve immediately. If storing, refrigerate in the Master Prep™ Pro Processing Bowl with lid on. Mousse will deflate over the course of several hours, but stored in the Master Prep™ Pro Processing Bowl itself, re-whipping will be a snap!

Dish into individual serving bowls and place into the freezer for 2 hours to create a light and fluffy frozen dessert that I would call Instant Ice Cream if making ice cream in the Ninja™ Master Prep™ Professional weren't so easy in its own right!

desserts

Pro Processing **Bowl**

Cherry **Mousse**

I don't know if I should, but I will admit to enjoying the flavor of artificial cherry flavoring once in a while… then you stop and realize that there really is nothing better than real cherry flavoring! If you've never had the chance to enjoy a dessert with the real thing in it, I highly recommend this delightful and simple mousse.

Shopping **List**

12 frozen cherries

1 ¼ cups heavy cream

2 ½ tablespoons sugar

¼ teaspoon vanilla extract

Directions

Serves **4**

❶ Place cherries in the Master Prep™ Pro Chopper. Secure the top and pulse 8-10 times until cherries are well juiced, but somewhat grainy. Set aside cherry mixture until step 3.

❷ Place heavy cream, sugar, and vanilla extract in the Master Prep™ Pro Processing Bowl. Secure the top and pulse in short bursts for 15-25 seconds, or until fluffy with strong peaks.

❸ Add cherry mixture into whipped cream mixture and pulse 5-7 more short pulses, until well combined. Serve immediately.

For an amazingly decadent dessert, whip up a batch of all three of my whipped desserts and serve a scoop of each, one on top of the other. Cherry Mousse on the bottom, topped with Chocolate Mousse, topped with Real Whipped Cream.

desserts

Whipped **Cream Cheese Frosting**

Really there are some baked goods that are simply not complete without a good Cream Cheese Frosting. Certainly, this is true for the fresh baked Carrot Cake, recipe page: 163, so try combining them for a truly perfect pairing.

Shopping **List**

8 ounces cream cheese (1 brick)

2 tablespoons butter

3 cups powdered sugar (about ¾ of a 1 pound box)

1 teaspoon vanilla extract

⅛ teaspoon salt

Serves **12**

Directions

❶ Place all ingredients in the Master Prep™ Pro Processing Bowl. Secure the top and pulse in 5 second bursts, until well combined and fluffy.

❷ Refrigerate for 1-2 hours to firm before frosting your favorite dessert. Keep your frosted, finished desserts refrigerated at all times.

desserts

Substitute 8 ounces of sour cream in place of the cream cheese for a homemade Sour Cream Frosting that is perfect to top cheesecakes, pastries or even cinnamon rolls!

 Pro **Pitcher**

Chocolate **Fudge**

Chocolate fudge has always been one of my favorite gifts to give friends and family at the holidays. With the most important thing about fudge being its melt in your mouth smooth texture, the Ninja™ Master Prep™ Professional is the perfect tool for the job! Lumps and clumps simply do not stand a chance.

Shopping **List**

½ cup butter

½ cup milk

2 cups light brown sugar

1 teaspoon vanilla extract

1 ½ cups dark chocolate chips

3 cups powdered sugar

Serves **32**

Directions

❶ Heat butter in a sauté pan over medium high heat until sizzling.

❷ Add milk and brown sugar to pan, stirring constantly. Bring to a boil and cook for 1 minute before removing from heat.

❸ Stir vanilla extract and chocolate into hot brown sugar mixture until fully combined. Let cool for 2-3 minutes until still hot, but not boiling hot.

❹ Place powdered sugar in the Master Prep™ Pro Pitcher and cover with chocolate and brown sugar mixture. Secure top and pulse for 10-15 seconds until smooth and fully combined.

❺ Pour finished fudge into an 8x8 baking dish for fudge squares or a small loaf pan for taller, thicker fudge. Refrigerate for at least 3 hours to firm up before slicing into 32 squares.

 For a Chocolate Pecan or Walnut Fudge: add in ¾ of a cup of pecans or walnuts after step 4, pulsing 3-4 times to roughly chop and combine.

desserts

 Pro **Pitcher**

Peanut **Butter Fudge**

Although chocolate is probably the all time classic fudge, peanut butter fudge is, and this may be surprising to hear coming from a chocolate fan like me, my favorite flavor of fudge. There is simply something irresistible about the densely packed nutty sweetness and smooth texture that I simply cannot refuse!

Shopping **List**

½ **cup butter**

½ **cup milk**

2 **cups light brown sugar**

1 **teaspoon vanilla extract**

1 **cup creamy peanut butter**

3 **cups powdered sugar**

Serves **32**

Directions

❶ Heat butter in a sauté pan over medium high heat until sizzling.

❷ Add milk and brown sugar to pan, stirring constantly. Bring to a boil and cook for 1 minute before removing from heat.

❸ Stir vanilla extract and peanut butter into hot brown sugar mixture until fully combined. Let cool for 2-3 minutes until still hot, but not boiling hot.

❹ Place powdered sugar in the Master Prep™ Pro Pitcher and cover with peanut butter and brown sugar mixture. Secure top and pulse for 10-15 seconds until smooth and fully combined.

❺ Pour finished fudge into an 8x8 baking dish for fudge squares or a small loaf pan for taller, thicker fudge. Refrigerate for at least 3 hours to firm up before slicing into 32 squares.

Bob's Tips

Peanut butter and chocolate make the perfect match, of course. Make a batch of Peanut Butter Fudge and a batch of my Chocolate Fudge, recipe page: 147 and package 2 squares of each as favors for your next party or get together. Both are pictured at left.

desserts

Pro **Chopper**

Marbled **Macadamia Bark**

This recipe for chocolate bark is sure to please! The semisweet and white chocolates marbled together is a treat for your eyes, but once you add the chopped macadamias on top… well, that's just a treat altogether.

Directions

1 Place macadamia nuts in Master Prep™ Pro Chopper. Secure Chopper's top and pulse 3-4 times, until nuts are roughly chopped.

Shopping **List**

1 cup macadamia nuts

1 ½ cups semisweet chocolate chips

1 ½ cups white chocolate chips

Serves **6**

2 Microwave semisweet chocolate chips for about 60-90 seconds, until melted, stopping at least once to stir.

3 Line a small sheet pan with wax paper, and then pour melted chocolate over top, tilting from side to side to coat the paper.

4 Microwave white chocolate chips for about 60-90 seconds, until melted, stopping at least once to stir.

5 Pour white chocolate directly over the semisweet chocolate, then use a wooden spatula to swirl and marble together. Sprinkle macadamia nuts over top.

6 Refrigerate for at least 3 hours to firm up before removing from pan and breaking into smaller pieces to serve.

 Bob's Tips

Homemade chocolate bark is probably the easiest, but impressive, gift you can give someone. I like to buy square tins and line them with wax paper, just don't forget the ribbon!

desserts

Pro Processing **Bowl**

Quick **and Easy Pie Crust**

A good crust is simply crucial when making a pie such as my Banana Cream Pie, recipe page: 157, or any pie really. If making a pie crust yourself has always seemed a little daunting, I recommend trying this recipe along with the help of the Ninja™ Master Prep™ Professional, and I'm sure it will be apparent why I decided to name this recipe "Quick and Easy Pie Crust."

Shopping List

1 ½ **cups all purpose flour**

3 **tablespoons milk**

½ **cup oil**

2 **teaspoons sugar**

1 **teaspoon salt**

Serves **8**

Directions

1 Preheat oven to 375 degrees.

2 Place all ingredients in the Master Prep™ Pro Processing Bowl. Secure Processing Bowl's top and pulse for 5 seconds, until all ingredients are well combined.

3 Press crust mixture evenly into the bottom and walls of a 9 inch pie pan. Bake for 10 minutes or until lightly browned.

4 Let cool for 30 minutes before refrigerating until use.

Bob's Tips

To bake up the most sturdy pie crust, cover unbaked crust with aluminum foil, pressing foil down into the crust until it is perfectly formed to the pan. Fill aluminum foil with heavy, raw beans before baking to keep pressure on crust as it bakes.

desserts

Pro Processing **Bowl**

Awesome **Brownies**

Making brownies from scratch is so easy, and thanks to the Ninja™ Master Prep™ Professional, making them perfectly lump-free is easier than ever! I like pecans in my brownies, which are simple to chop in the Master Prep™ Pro Chopper as you prepare the brownie batter in the Pro Processing Bowl.

Directions

❶ Preheat oven to 350 degrees. Place butter in Master Prep™ Pro Processing Bowl (without blades in place) and microwave on high for 45-60 seconds, until melted.

❷ Insert blades and add cocoa powder to the melted butter. Secure top and pulse in 7 short bursts, or until well combined.

❸ Add sugar, brown sugar, flour, baking powder, eggs, and vanilla extract to the cocoa mixture and re-secure top. Pulse in 7-10 long bursts, or until well combined and free of lumps.

❹ Add pecans to the Master Prep™ Pro Chopper and secure top. Pulse in 5 short bursts, just until pecans are lightly chopped.

❺ Carefully remove blades from Processing Bowl and stir in chopped pecans and chocolate chips with a long spoon. Pour batter into an 8x8 baking dish sprayed with nonstick cooking spray. Bake for 30-35 minutes, or until a toothpick inserted into the center comes out mostly clean. Slice into 9 squares to serve.

Shopping **List**

¾ **cup butter or margarine**
½ **cup cocoa powder**
¾ **cup sugar**
¼ **cup light brown sugar**
1 **cup flour**
¾ **teaspoon baking powder**
2 **large eggs**
1 **teaspoon vanilla extract**
1 **cup pecans**
¾ **cup semisweet chocolate chips**
nonstick cooking spray

Serves **9**

Walnuts can be substituted in place of the pecans, or try using peanuts and substituting peanut butter morsels in place of the chocolate chips for Peanut Butter Cup Brownies!

desserts

 Pro **Pitcher**

Chocolate **Chip Pound Cake**

I have never had any luck baking pound cake from scratch! Thankfully, I've always had very, very good luck baking this pound cake, which starts from a box of ordinary yellow cake mix. Though it isn't completely from scratch, using extra eggs, milk and butter in place of the water and oil of typical cake mix really makes this into a true pound cake!

Shopping **List**

1 box (18.25 ounces) yellow cake mix

1 box (3.4 ounces) instant vanilla pudding mix

1 cup butter or margarine, softened

4 large eggs

1 cup milk

1 ½ cups semi-sweet chocolate chips

confectioners sugar, for garnish

Serves **12**

Directions

1 Preheat oven to 325 degrees.

2 Place cake mix, pudding mix, butter, eggs, and milk in the Master Prep™ Pro Pitcher, secure the top, and pulse in 10 long pulses (about 1 minute all together). Use a rubber spatula the scrape down the walls of the pitcher and then pulse a few more times, until batter is smooth and lump free.

3 Remove blades and use a rubber spatula to fold the chocolate chips into the batter.

4 Pour batter into a 12 cup Bundt or tube pan and bake for 60-65 minutes, or until a toothpick inserted into the center comes out mostly clean.

5 Cool completely before dusting with confectioners sugar and slicing to serve.

 It may not seem like all of the ingredients will fit into the pitcher at first, but I promise you that they will!

desserts

Pro Processing **Bowl**

Graham **Cracker Pie Crust**

A good graham cracker pie crust is the perfect base for many different pies, my favorites being for a Creamy Key Lime Pie, recipe page: 160, or a chocolate cream pie. Substitute chocolate flavored graham crackers in place of the cinnamon ones for an even better match to a chocolate cream pie.

Shopping **List**

1 ½ **cups graham crackers**

3 **tablespoons butter or margarine**

3 **tablespoons sugar**

Serves **8**

Directions

❶ Preheat oven to 375 degrees.

❷ Place graham crackers, butter and sugar in the Master Prep™ Pro Processing Bowl. Secure Processing Bowl's top and pulse for 10 seconds, until cookies are entirely pulverized.

❸ Press cookie mixture evenly into the bottom and walls of a 9 inch pie pan. Bake for 8 minutes.

❹ Let cool for 30 minutes before refrigerating until use.

 This works best with slightly softened, but not melted butter. When making a very sweet pie, there's no need to add the additional sugar.

desserts

 Pro **Pitcher**

Banana **Cream Pie**

This recipe for Banana Cream Pie is so creamy and so easy that you may be surprised by just how much flavor that it packs! Traditionally prepared with a double boiler on the stove and a whole lot of whisking, this recipe doesn't even require a stove!

Directions

❶ Prepare, bake and cool one Quick and Easy Pie Crust, according to the directions on that page. Set out non-dairy whipped topping to thaw for about 10 minutes.

❷ Place vanilla pudding mix, milk, 1 peeled banana (reserving the other 2 for step 5), and banana extract in Master Prep™ Pro Pitcher. Secure top and pulse for 15-20 seconds, until creamy and lump free.

❸ Pour banana and pudding mixture into a large mixing bowl and gently fold non-dairy whipped topping into it with a rubber spatula, just until the two are combined. Do not over mix or the whipped topping will collapse!

❹ Pour the finished pie filling into the Quick and Easy Pie Crust and refrigerate for at least 2 hours, until set.

❺ Peel and slice the remaining 2 bananas into ¼ inch slices. Arrange the slices on top of the set cream filling in an even layer. Garnish with an entire, thick layer of whipped cream and serve immediately.

Shopping **List**

1 Quick and Easy Pie Crust, recipe page: 151

1 tub (8 ounces) non-dairy whipped topping

1 box (3.4 ounces) instant vanilla pudding mix

1 ½ cups milk

3 bananas

½ teaspoon banana extract

whipped cream, to top

Serves **8**

 Bob's Tips — To keep the fresh, sliced bananas that top this pie from turning brown, you may want to dip them in a small glass of water mixed with 1 tablespoon lemon juice. The trick to cutting the perfect slice is to add the top whipped cream layer after the pie is sliced and on serving plates.

desserts

Pro Processing **Bowl**

Baked **Meringue Cookies**

Since the Ninja™ Master Prep™ Professional really does most of the work in this recipe, be careful that you don't forget they're in the oven as they bake for a very long time at a very low temperature to crisp up without burning. Trust me, they're known as "forgotten cookies" for a reason!

Directions

❶ Preheat oven to 200 degrees and line a baking sheet with parchment paper.

Shopping **List**

3 large egg whites

¼ teaspoon cream of tartar

¾ cup sugar

½ teaspoon vanilla extract

Serves **8**

❷ Place egg whites and cream of tartar in the Master Prep™ Pro Processing Bowl. Secure the top and pulse in 15 second intervals for about 90 seconds, or until egg whites are nearly strong enough to cling to an upside down spoon.

❸ Open the Master Prep™ Pro Processing Bowl's pour spout and pour in about ¼ of the sugar, and all of the vanilla extract. Pulse for 10 seconds, and then pour in another ¼ of the sugar. Repeat until sugar is fully combined and then pulse an additional 20 seconds. Meringue should be forming stiff peaks (that stay formed).

❹ Use a teaspoon to spoon small, quarter sized lumps of the meringue onto a baking sheet about an inch apart. (You may have enough meringue to fill 2 baking sheets!)

❺ Bake for 80-90 minutes, until cookies do not give when you poke them. Crack oven door and let cookies cool, in oven, for 2 hours before serving.

Use a pastry bag with various pastry tips to create unique and beautiful meringue cookies. Various extracts and food colorings may be added in step 3 to completely change their look and flavor!

desserts

Pro **Pitcher**

Creamy **Key Lime Pie**

Somewhere in between a key lime pie and a key lime cheesecake, my Creamy Key Lime Pie still has the delectable tart flavoring that you'd expect from any key lime dessert. It's only lacking in one thing… classification.

Directions

1 Preheat oven to 350 degrees and place pie crust, in pie pan, on a baking sheet.

2 Place cream cheese, sweetened condensed milk, egg, egg yolks, key lime juice and sugar in Master Prep™ Pro Pitcher. Secure top and pulse for 15-20 seconds, until creamy and well combined.

3 Pour pie filling into crust and shake crust to settle. Bake for 12 minutes.

4 Remove from oven and let cool for 1 hour before refrigerating for at least 2 hours. Serve chilled, topped with whipped cream and a slice of fresh key lime.

Shopping **List**

1 Graham Cracker Pie Crust, recipe page: 156

8 ounces cream cheese (1 brick)

1 can (14 ounces) sweetened condensed milk

1 large egg

2 large egg yolks

½ cup key lime juice

1 tablespoon sugar

whipped cream, for garnish

Serves **8**

Bob's Tips

Key lime juice is an absolute must for key lime pie, as it has an entirely different flavor than regular lime juice. You can, however, make a creamy lemon pie by substituting fresh lemon juice and ½ teaspoon of lemon extract.

desserts

 Pro **Pitcher**

Peanut **Butter Cookies**

Whenever I'm in the mood for a sweet comfort food, a hot fresh batch of Peanut Butter Cookies is the first thing that comes to mind. They really are incredibly simple to make, and best served right out of the oven, so skip the store bought ones and try this traditional recipe!

Shopping **List**

nonstick cooking spray
⅔ **cup peanut butter**
½ **cup butter or margarine, softened**
1 **large egg**
⅔ **cup sugar**
⅓ **cup light brown sugar**
½ **teaspoon vanilla extract**
1 ¼ **cups all purpose flour**
1 **teaspoon baking soda**
¼ **teaspoon salt**

Serves **12**

Directions

❶ Preheat oven to 375 degrees and spray a baking sheet with nonstick cooking spray.

❷ Place peanut butter, butter, egg, sugar, brown sugar and vanilla extract in Master Prep™ Pro Pitcher. Secure top and pulse for 10 seconds, until well combined.

❸ Add flour, baking soda and salt to the peanut butter mixture and re-secure top. Pulse for 15-20 seconds until cookie dough is smooth and lump free.

❹ Carefully remove blades from Pitcher, and then scoop out cookie dough, one rounded tablespoon at a time. Use your palms to form into perfectly round balls, and then drop onto the greased baking sheet about 1 ½ inches apart. (You may have enough dough to fill two sheet pans!)

❺ Press cookies down with a fork, first vertically, then horizontally, to create the classic, woven look of peanut butter cookies that also promotes even baking. Bake for 10 minutes for chewy cookies and 12-14 minutes for crispy. Makes about 24 cookies.

 For chunky peanut butter cookies: Pulse ½ cup of roasted peanuts in the Master Prep™ Pro Chopper, just 2-3 times until chopped. Add chopped peanuts to dough right before forming cookies, or sprinkle over top before pressing down with a fork.

desserts

 Pro **Pitcher**

Carrot **Cake**

This Carrot Cake is so moist and flavorful, with tiny bits of real fresh carrots that no box of cake mix could ever even come close to replicating. Just don't let a rabbit anywhere near it!

Directions

1 Preheat oven to 350 degrees. Place carrots in Master Prep™ Pro Pitcher. Secure top and pulse for 10 seconds, until carrots are grated into tiny pieces. Remove carrots and set aside.

2 Place vegetable oil, sugar and eggs in Master Prep™ Pro Pitcher. Secure top and pulse for 10 seconds, until combined and frothy.

Shopping **List**

1 ½ cups baby carrots
1 cup vegetable oil
1 ⅓ cups sugar
3 large eggs
1 ⅓ cups flour
1 ½ teaspoons baking soda
¼ teaspoon salt
1 rounded teaspoon cinnamon
1 teaspoon vanilla extract
1 batch Whipped Cream Cheese Frosting, recipe page: 146

Serves **8**

3 Add flour, baking soda, salt, cinnamon and vanilla extract to the sugar mixture in Pitcher and re-secure top. Pulse for 10 seconds until well combined and free of lumps.

4 Carefully remove blades from Pitcher and stir in grated carrots with a long spoon. Pour finished cake batter into two, greased and floured 8 inch cake pans. Bake for 30 minutes or until a toothpick inserted into the center comes out clean.

5 Let cool for at least 1 hour. Use a bread knife to slice off each half of the cake's rounded tops for a perfectly flat, bakery style cake. Frost each top with Cream Cheese Frosting, and then flip one on top of the other to let the frosting of each half glue the cake together. Frost the outside of the cake, decorate and serve.

I like to add ½ cup raisins in step 5 to make this cake even better! To make carrot decorations: most stores sell small tubes of green and orange icing, as well as pastry tips that fit right onto the tube.

 Pro **Pitcher**

White **Chocolate Raspberry Cupcakes**

The Ninja™ Master Prep™ Professional is pulling double duty on these beautiful and unique cupcakes. Not only does it help make the batter light and fluffy, it also purees fresh raspberries for the frosting.

Directions

1 Preheat oven to 350 degrees. Place cake mix, pudding mix, water, butter, vegetable oil, and egg whites in the Master Prep™ Pro Pitcher, secure the top, and pulse in 10 long pulses (about 1 minute all together). Use a rubber spatula the scrape down the walls of the pitcher and then pulse a few more times, until batter is smooth and lump free.

Shopping **List**

1 box (18.25 ounces) white cake mix
1 box (3.4 ounces) instant white chocolate pudding mix
1 ⅓ cups water
2 tablespoons butter, melted
1 tablespoon vegetable oil
3 large egg whites
½ cup raspberries
⅔ cup confectioners sugar
1 container white frosting
white chocolate chips

Serves **18**

2 Use the batter to fill 18-24 cupcakes, lined with paper liners, about 2/3 of the way full.

3 Bake for 20-25 minutes, or until a toothpick inserted into the center of a cupcake comes out mostly clean. Let cool completely.

4 Place raspberries and confectioners sugar in the Master Prep™ Pro Processing bowl, secure the top, and pulse in 7 long pulses, until completely blended. Remove blades and use a rubber spatula to gently fold frosting into raspberry mixture. Refrigerate until ready to ice cupcakes.

5 Use a pastry bag or icing spatula to ice cupcakes with the raspberry frosting. Top each with a few white chocolate chips before serving.

 Bob's Tips

The raspberry candies (sold in most stores with a large candy section) shown in the photograph to the left make a really great garnish for these cupcakes, but fresh raspberries work really well too! Also shown is clear edible cake glitter, sold in the baking sections of craft stores.

desserts

Pro **Pitcher**

Almond **Coconut Macaroons**

These macaroons are not your ordinary coconut cookies. The use of ground almonds as a base, rather than dry flour, keeps the cookies as moist as can be while giving the macaroons a slightly nutty sweetness.

Directions

❶ Preheat oven to 325 degrees and spray a baking sheet with nonstick cooking spray.

❷ Place almonds, sugar and salt in the Master Prep™ Pro Pitcher. Secure Pitcher's top and pulse 15-20 seconds until almonds are a well grated, breadcrumb consistency.

❸ Add egg whites, vanilla extract and coconut flakes to the ground almonds and re-secure top. Pulse only 4-5 times until ingredients are well combined, but coconut is still somewhat intact.

❹ Carefully remove blades from Pitcher, and then scoop out mixture, one very rounded teaspoon at a time. Drop onto the greased baking sheet about an inch apart. Bake for 18-20 minutes, until a golden brown. Makes about 24 cookies.

Shopping **List**

nonstick cooking spray

1 cup almonds

½ **cup sugar**

¼ **teaspoon salt**

3 large egg whites

1 teaspoon vanilla extract

2 ⅔ cups sweetened coconut flakes

Serves **12**

Bob's Tips

For stringier, chewier macaroons; do not add coconut in step 3. Add the coconut after the other ingredients are well mixed and use a spoon to combine.

desserts

Pro **Pitcher**

Frozen Chocolate Custard

While this frozen custard isn't the kind of recipe you'd make every day, this is about as real as it gets, and it makes a great indulgence to scratch off your bucket list!

Directions

❶ Place sugar, salt and egg yolks in the Master Prep™ Pro Pitcher. Pulse for 15-20 seconds, until yolks thicken slightly.

❷ In a medium sauce pan, heat half and half over medium heat until simmering. Fill a large pot with water. Take simmering half and half off of the heat and replace with the pot of water. Turn heat up to high until boiling. Reduce to medium high.

❸ Transfer hot half and half into a pourable container, such as a gravy boat. Open the pour spout on the Master Prep™ Pro Pitcher and pulse the egg yolk mixture as you slowly pour in the hot half and half until fully combined.

❹ Pour combined egg yolk, and half and half mixture back into the medium sauce pan, add the chocolate chips, and place pan over the pot of boiling water. Stir constantly to prevent boiling until the custard fully coats the back of a spoon.

❺ Pour custard through a strainer and back into the Master Prep™ Pro Pitcher. Allow to cool for 5 minutes before adding heavy cream and vanilla extract. Secure the Pitcher's top and pulse 4-5 times until combined.

❻ Pour custard into two ice cube trays and freeze for at least 5 hours.

❼ Place frozen custard cubes in Master Prep™ Pro Pitcher. Secure Pitcher's top and pulse for 15-20 seconds until smooth and creamy. Serve immediately or freeze for 15-20 minutes for a harder consistency.

Shopping List

1 cup sugar
¼ teaspoon salt
7 large egg yolks
1 ½ cups half and half
⅓ cup semisweet chocolate chips
1 cup heavy cream
½ teaspoon vanilla extract

Serves **5**

To make Vanilla Frozen Custard: Simply omit the chocolate chips and add up the vanilla extract to 3 teaspoons.

ice creams

Pro **Pitcher**

Double Strawberry Ice Cream

Though the texture of the ice creams in this book are closer to soft serve than traditional ice cream, I've found that the thick and freezing texture of frozen strawberries really helps thicken things up, while also making things that much more delicious, of course!

Shopping List

1 ½ cups plus ½ cup milk
¼ cup heavy whipping cream
¼ cup sugar
1 cup frozen strawberries
1 tablespoon strawberry syrup
¼ teaspoon vanilla extract

Serves **3**

Directions

❶ Combine 1 ½ cups of the milk, whipping cream and sugar, and then stir to dissolve sugar. Fill one 16 cube ice cube tray with the mixture. Freeze for at least 3 hours, or until frozen solid.

❷ Place ice cream cubes in the Master Prep™ Pro Pitcher and then add frozen strawberries, strawberry syrup, vanilla extract and the remaining ½ cup of milk over top. Secure the Pitcher's top and pulse for 10-15 seconds, until smooth and creamy.

❸ Serve garnished with a drizzle of strawberry syrup or fresh strawberries.

The strawberry syrup in this recipe refers to the squeeze bottle syrup used for making strawberry milk, not the sticky strawberry sauce sold for making strawberry shortcake. While strawberry syrup tends to taste a little artificial, strawberry sauce tends to taste like… well, not much at all.

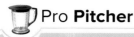 Pro **Pitcher**

Banana **Chocolate Chip Ice Cream**

Despite being sweet in their own right, I find that chocolate chips calm down the extreme level of sweetness in a ripe banana, and therefore they combine to make a perfectly balanced ice cream flavor. Anytime I have any bananas that are on the overripe side, I throw them in the freezer so that I'm prepared the next time I want a batch.

Shopping **List**

1 ½ cups plus ½ cup milk

¼ cup heavy whipping cream

¼ cup sugar

1 banana, peeled and frozen

½ teaspoon banana extract

¼ cup chocolate chips

Serves **3**

Directions

❶ Combine 1 ½ cups of the milk, whipping cream and sugar, and stir to dissolve sugar. Fill one 16 cube ice cube tray with the mixture. Freeze for at least 3 hours, or until frozen solid.

❷ Place ice cream cubes in the Master Prep™ Pro Pitcher and then add frozen banana, banana extract and the remaining ½ cup of milk over top. Secure the Pitcher's top and pulse for 10-15 seconds, until smooth and creamy.

❸ Add chocolate chips to ice cream and re-secure top. Pulse 3 times, until chocolate chips are roughly chopped and dispersed throughout.

❹ Serve garnished with additional chocolate chips and a fresh slice of banana.

 Bob's Tips

For something a little different: try making this recipe with white chocolate chips and ¼ cup of macadamia nuts, adding them in step 3.

ice creams

Pro **Pitcher**

Smores' Ice Cream

I thought up this recipe when a craving for the campfire classic hit me but I realized there was no way I was lighting a fire of any kind in the summer heat. The only problem is, now I have a new dilemma of figuring out what to do when the craving for this Smores' Ice Cream hits when I'm out camping….

Shopping **List**

1 ½ **cups plus** ½ **cup milk**

¼ **cup heavy whipping cream**

¼ **cup sugar**

2 **tablespoons chocolate syrup**

2 **cinnamon graham crackers**

mini marshmallows, for garnish

Serves **3**

Directions

❶ Combine 1 ½ cups of the milk, whipping cream and sugar, and then stir to dissolve sugar. Fill one 16 cube ice cube tray with the mixture. Freeze for at least 3 hours, or until frozen solid.

❷ Place ice cream cubes in the Master Prep™ Pro Pitcher and then add chocolate syrup and remaining ½ cup milk over top. Secure the Pitcher's top and pulse for 10-15 seconds, until smooth and creamy.

❸ Add graham crackers and re-secure top. Pulse 5-7 times until graham crackers are broken up and dispersed throughout.

❹ Serve garnished with mini marshmallows, a whole graham cracker and a drizzle of chocolate syrup.

For a different take on presentation: serve garnished with a dollop of marshmallow fluff and chocolate chips.

ice creams

 Pro **Pitcher**

Chocolate Coconut Ice Cream

Many may not know that an older alternative spelling for coconut is cocoanut. I wonder if whoever gave it that name had any idea just how perfectly coconut and chocolate go together— because as this ice cream demonstrates, they are a flawless match!

Directions

❶ Combine milk, whipping cream, vanilla extract and sugar, stirring to dissolve sugar. Fill one 16 cube ice cube tray with the mixture. Freeze for at least 3 hours, or until frozen solid.

Shopping List

1 ½ cups milk

¼ cup heavy whipping cream

½ teaspoon vanilla extract

3 tablespoons sugar

4 tablespoons chocolate syrup

⅓ cup coconut milk

1 tablespoon shredded coconut

Serves **3**

❷ Place ice cream cubes in the Master Prep™ Pro Pitcher and then add chocolate syrup and coconut milk over top. Secure the Pitcher's top and pulse for 10-15 seconds, until smooth and creamy.

❸ Add shredded coconut and re-secure top. Pulse 5-7 times until shredded coconut is finely minced and dispersed throughout.

❹ Serve garnished with toasted coconut and a square of chocolate.

 Bob's Tips

Regular milk and ½ a teaspoon of coconut extract may be used in place of the coconut milk in a pinch. Add a tablespoon of chocolate chips and 3 tablespoons of marshmallows in with the shredded coconut for a Coconut Rocky Road Ice Cream.

ice creams

Pro **Pitcher**

Mocha **Madness Ice Cream**

This recipe for mocha flavored ice cream makes a fantastic dessert after dinner, but be sure to keep in mind that the recipe calls for a cup of double strength coffee! If having caffeine later in the day tends to keep you up at night, make sure to use decaffeinated coffee.

Shopping **List**

1 ½ **cups milk**

¼ **cup heavy whipping cream**

¼ **cup sugar**

½ **cup coffee, double strength, chilled**

2 **tablespoons chocolate syrup**

Serves **3**

Directions

❶ Combine milk, whipping cream and sugar, and then stir to dissolve sugar. Fill one 16 cube ice cube tray with the mixture. Freeze for at least 3 hours, or until frozen solid.

❷ Place ice cream cubes in the Master Prep™ Pro Pitcher and then add coffee and chocolate syrup over top. Secure the Pitcher's top and pulse for 10-15 seconds, until smooth and creamy.

❸ Serve garnished with a drizzle of chocolate syrup or chocolate covered espresso beans.

I don't prefer running brewed coffee back through a coffee maker a second time and have instead found that the best way to make extra strong coffee is to simply cut the brewing process short and "catch" the first ½ cup of coffee brewed from a full pot of grounds.

ice creams

 Pro **Pitcher**

Cherry **Chocolate Chunk**

Though there are many varieties of store-bought ice cream that include chocolate chips or chunks, I've always found the texture of the chocolate in these ice creams to pale in comparison to any chocolate bar on the shelf. Thanks to the Ninja™ Master Prep™ Professional, now you can use any chocolate you wish, however dark you prefer!

Directions

❶ Combine 1 ½ cups of the milk, whipping cream, and sugar and stir to dissolve sugar. Fill one 16 cube ice cube tray with the mixture. Freeze for at least 3 hours, or until frozen solid.

❷ Place ice cream cubes in the Master Prep™ Pro Pitcher and then add vanilla extract and the remaining ½ cup of milk over top. Secure the Pitcher's top and pulse for 10 seconds, until almost smooth.

❸ Add frozen cherries and dark chocolate to ice cream and re-secure top. Pulse 4-7 times, until cherries and chocolate are roughly chopped and dispersed throughout.

❹ Serve garnished with a fresh cherry or drizzled with chocolate syrup.

Shopping **List**

1 ½ cups plus ½ cup milk

¼ cup heavy whipping cream

¼ cup sugar

¼ teaspoon vanilla extract

¾ cup frozen cherries

4-6 squares dark chocolate

Serves **3**

 Bob's Tips

Frozen cherries are the easiest way to make this recipe, as they are already pitted, but you can pit and use fresh if you prefer. For best results, you should still freeze the fresh for at least an hour before preparing.

ice creams

Pro **Pitcher**

Caramel **Nut Ice Cream**

I have always loved this ice cream for its smooth flavors and its crunchy texture. Fold in ribbons of thick caramel syrup and top with whipped cream and chocolate syrup for a decadent caramel sundae.

Directions

1 Combine 1 ½ cups of the milk, whipping cream, vanilla extract and sugar, and then stir to dissolve sugar. Fill one 16 cube ice cube tray with the mixture. Freeze for at least 3 hours, or until frozen solid.

Shopping **List**

1 ½ cups plus ½ cup milk

¼ cup heavy whipping cream

½ teaspoon vanilla extract

¼ cup sugar

3 tablespoons caramel syrup

⅛ teaspoon salt

¼ cup pecans

Serves **3**

2 Place ice cream cubes in the Master Prep™ Pro Pitcher and then add caramel syrup, salt and remaining ½ cup milk over top. Secure the Pitcher's top and pulse for 10-15 seconds, until smooth and creamy.

3 Add pecans and re-secure top. Pulse 5-7 times until pecans are broken up and dispersed throughout.

4 Serve garnished with a drizzle of caramel syrup or a square of caramel candy.

 Bob's Tips

Salt and caramel go fantastically well together… while the French would probably frown upon this method of making ice cream, they certainly wouldn't argue with that! Personally I like to use ¼ a teaspoon of salt in caramel ice cream, but you should probably taste as you go, adding a tiny pinch at a time.

ice creams

Pro **Pitcher**

Orange **Sherbert**

Of all the many ways to enjoy the combination of oranges and cream, a good sherbert has got to be my absolute favorite. It is simply so decadent, yet refreshing, that I love to slowly savor every spoonful on a balmy day.

Shopping **List**

1 ½ cups plus ½ cup milk

¼ cup heavy whipping cream

3 tablespoons sugar

4 tablespoons frozen orange juice concentrate

Serves **3**

Directions

1 Combine 1 ½ cups of the milk, whipping cream and sugar, and stir to dissolve sugar. Fill one 16 cube ice cube tray with the mixture. Freeze for at least 3 hours, or until frozen solid.

2 Place ice cream cubes in the Master Prep™ Pro Pitcher and then add frozen orange juice concentrate and the remaining ½ cup of milk over top. Secure the Pitcher's top and pulse for 10-15 seconds, until smooth and creamy.

3 Serve garnished with a vanilla cookie or a pinch of orange zest.

Bob's Tips

For less of a soft serve texture and more of a thick, almost gelato like consistency: transfer into individual serving dishes and freeze for 30 minutes, until almost entirely solidified.

ice creams

 Pro **Pitcher**

Strawberry **Frozen Yogurt**

One of the great things I have found about the Ninja™ Master Prep™ Professional is that it can turn normal yogurt into a delicious frozen dessert with very little effort. Feel free to experiment with different fruits or yogurts, all you need to do is pick the flavor and let the Ninja™ Master Prep™ Professional do the work!

Shopping **List**

2 cups plus ½ cup vanilla yogurt

2 cups frozen strawberries

4 teaspoons sugar or 2 packets sugar substitute

Serves **5**

Directions

❶ Fill a 16 cube ice cube tray with 2 cups of the vanilla yogurt. Freeze for at least 3 hours, or until frozen solid.

❷ Place yogurt cubes, frozen strawberries, sugar and the remaining ½ cup of vanilla yogurt in the Master Prep™ Pro Pitcher. Secure the top and pulse for 10-20 seconds, until smooth and creamy.

❸ Serve garnished with a fresh strawberry or whipped cream. If yogurt softens or you prefer a thicker texture, place the finished frozen yogurt in freezer for 20 minutes to harden before serving.

 Bob's Tips

For something a little different, substitute light brown sugar for the regular sugar in this recipe. For an even more intense strawberry taste, simply substitute strawberry yogurt in place of the vanilla. Try using cheesecake flavored yogurt for Strawberry Cheesecake Frozen Yogurt.

ice creams

Pro Pitcher

Blueberry Cinnamon Bun Frozen Yogurt

Making a good blueberry frozen yogurt has always been one of my favorite ways to enjoy blueberries as the flavor of the berries by themselves, often varying greatly in flavor from sweet to tart, is unified and smoothed out. Blueberries are most abundant in the summer months, so I recommend stocking up as they are easy to freeze and hold well.

Shopping List

2 cups plus ½ cup vanilla yogurt

1 ½ cups frozen blueberries

4 teaspoons light brown sugar or 2 packets sugar substitute

½ teaspoon ground cinnamon

Serves **5**

Directions

1 Fill a 16 cube ice cube tray with 2 cups of the vanilla yogurt. Freeze for at least 3 hours, or until frozen solid.

2 Place yogurt cubes, frozen blueberries, brown sugar, cinnamon and the remaining ½ cup of vanilla yogurt in the Master Prep™ Pro Pitcher. Secure the top and pulse for 10-20 seconds, until smooth and creamy.

3 Serve garnished with fresh blueberries or whipped cream. If yogurt softens or you prefer a thicker texture, place the finished frozen yogurt in freezer for 20 minutes to harden before serving.

Bob's Tips

To create an extra blueberry ribbon in your frozen yogurt, try heating a handful of fresh blueberries and a tablespoon of sugar on the stove over medium heat, macerating them with a spoon until nearly liquefied. Let cool for 5 minutes before using a knife to swirl throughout the frozen yogurt.

ice creams

Chocolate **Covered Raspberry Frozen Yogurt**

If you've learned anything about me from this cookbook, you know that chocolate and raspberries are some of my favorite things; so I had to include this recipe for one of my favorite frozen yogurt flavors. Luckily, for any of you strawberry or blueberry lovers, this recipe can easily be altered to use some of your favorite things.

Shopping **List**

2 cups plus ½ cup vanilla yogurt

1 ½ cups frozen raspberries

3 tablespoons chocolate syrup

Serves **5**

Directions

❶ Fill a 16 cube ice cube tray with 2 cups of the vanilla yogurt. Freeze for at least 3 hours, or until frozen solid.

❷ Place yogurt cubes, frozen raspberries, chocolate syrup and the remaining ½ cup of vanilla yogurt in the Master Prep™ Pro Pitcher. Secure the top and pulse for 10-20 seconds, until smooth and creamy.

❸ Serve garnished with fresh raspberries, shaved chocolate, a drizzle of chocolate syrup or whipped cream. If yogurt softens or you prefer a thicker texture, place the finished frozen yogurt in freezer for 20 minutes to harden before serving.

Bob's Tips

To make a Raspberry Chocolate Chip Frozen Yogurt: substitute ¼ cup of dark chocolate pieces in place of the chocolate syrup and add 2 teaspoons of sugar to make up for the sugar of the syrup.

ice creams

Pro **Pitcher**

Pumpkin **Pecan Frozen Yogurt**

With their extensive growing range and versatility, pumpkins have been widely used well before they were ever associated with Halloween or Thanksgiving. Basically, what I'm saying is that you shouldn't let the time of year stop you from enjoying the uniquely wonderful flavor that pumpkin offers. But of course, this frozen yogurt really is a great Fall treat that makes a great addition to Thanksgiving dinner as well!

Shopping **List**

2 cups plus ½ cup vanilla yogurt

2 cups canned pumpkin, chilled

4 teaspoons light brown sugar or 2 packets sugar substitute

1 teaspoon pumpkin pie spice

¼ cup pecans, shelled

Serves **5**

Directions

1 Fill a 16 cube ice cube tray with 2 cups of the vanilla yogurt. Freeze for at least 3 hours, or until frozen solid.

2 Place yogurt cubes, pumpkin, brown sugar, pumpkin pie spice and the remaining ½ cup of vanilla yogurt in the Master Prep™ Pro Pitcher. Secure the top and pulse for 10-20 seconds, until smooth and creamy.

3 Add pecans to the frozen yogurt, re-secure the Pitcher's top and pulse an additional 3-4 times until roughly chopped and combined throughout.

4 Serve garnished with a whole pecan or whipped cream. If yogurt softens or you prefer a thicker texture, place the finished frozen yogurt in freezer for 20 minutes to harden before serving.

When shopping for canned pumpkin, be sure to buy unsweetened pumpkin and not prepared pumpkin pie filling. If pumpkin pie filling is all that is available, that may also be used as long as you omit the brown sugar and pumpkin pie spice.

ice creams

Strawberry Sorbet

D on't let the ingredients of this sweet and refreshing recipe catch you off guard. The vodka—which I promise you'd be hard pressed to taste—stops too many ice crystals from forming and the sorbet from freezing solid, allowing it to stay creamy without any dairy! Just make sure you read my tip below before preparing this dish for any children.

Shopping List

½ cup sugar
⅓ cup water
2 cups fresh strawberries, hulled
1 tablespoon lemon juice
1 tablespoon vodka (for smoothest consistency, optional)

Serves **3**

Directions

❶ Place sugar and water in a sauce pan over medium heat, stirring constantly, just until sugar dissolves. Let cool for 20 minutes.

❷ Place strawberries, lemon juice, vodka, and cooled sugar mixture in the Master Prep™ Pro Pitcher. Secure the Pitcher's top and pulse for 20 seconds, until extremely smooth. If you own an ice cream maker, stop here and follow the directions for your model; if you do not, continue to step 3.

❸ Pour sorbet mixture into a large baking dish or deep sheet pan. Cover dish or pan with aluminum foil and place in freezer for 3-4 hours, until nearly frozen solid. If you'd prefer, you may serve the sorbet at this stage by running an ice cream scoop down the length of the dish to scrape together a nice, full scoop. For an even more solid, yet still creamy consistency, continue to step 4.

❹ Use a metal spatula to scrape the nearly frozen sorbet out of the pan in large chunks. Place these chunks back into the Master Prep™ Pro Pitcher. Secure the Pitcher's top and pulse for 15 seconds, until extremely smooth and creamy. Transfer this finished sorbet mixture into any airtight container and freeze overnight before serving.

 If serving to children: you can keep the creaminess and lose the alcohol by dissolving ¼ of a packet of strawberry flavored gelatin into the sugar and water mixture in step 1. Only let cool for 5 minutes instead of 20, stirring occasionally, as gelatin lumps may form.

ice creams

Pro **Pitcher**

Mango **Sorbet**

Offering an understated yet distinct flavor, mangoes are an ideal base for a tropical sorbet. For a special treat, I particularly enjoy it with a drizzling of strawberry syrup.

Directions

1 Place sugar and water in a sauce pan over medium heat, stirring constantly, just until sugar dissolves. Let cool for 20 minutes.

2 Place mango, lime juice, light rum, and cooled sugar mixture in the Master Prep™ Pro Pitcher. Secure the Pitcher's top and pulse for 20 seconds, until extremely smooth. If you own an ice cream maker, stop here and follow the directions for your model; if you do not, continue to step 3.

3 Pour sorbet mixture into a large baking dish or deep sheet pan. Cover dish or pan with aluminum foil and place in freezer for 3-4 hours, until nearly frozen solid. If you'd prefer, you may serve the sorbet at this stage by running an ice cream scoop down the length of the dish to scrape together a nice, full scoop. For an even more solid, yet still creamy consistency, continue to step 4.

4 Use a metal spatula to scrape the nearly frozen sorbet out of the pan in large chunks. Place these chunks back into the Master Prep™ Pro Pitcher. Secure the Pitcher's top and pulse for 15 seconds, until extremely smooth and creamy. Transfer this finished sorbet mixture into any airtight container and freeze overnight before serving.

Shopping **List**

½ **cup sugar**
⅓ **cup water**
2 cups fresh mango, peeled and pitted
1 ½ tablespoons lime juice
1 tablespoon light rum (for smoothest consistency, optional)

Serves **3**

If serving to children: you can keep the creaminess and lose the alcohol by dissolving ¼ of a packet of tropical fruit flavored gelatin into the sugar and water mixture in step 1. Only let cool for 5 minutes instead of 20, stirring occasionally, as gelatin lumps may form.

ice creams

Pro **Pitcher**

Melon Sorbet

I imagine that the reason you don't find a lot of melon flavored ice creams is that the cream base overpowers the subtle sweetness of the melon. I also imagine that that is why melons make a wonderful base for a sorbet, as they themselves are the base.

Directions

❶ Place sugar and water in a sauce pan over medium heat, stirring constantly, just until sugar dissolves. Let cool for 20 minutes.

Shopping **List**

½ **cup sugar**
⅓ **cup water**
1 cup fresh cantaloupe chunks
1 cup fresh honeydew chunks
2 tablespoons pineapple juice
1 tablespoon vodka (for smoothest consistency, optional)

Serves **3**

❷ Place cantaloupe, honeydew, pineapple juice, vodka, and cooled sugar mixture in the Master Prep™ Pro Pitcher. Secure the Pitcher's top and pulse for 20 seconds, until extremely smooth. If you own an ice cream maker, stop here and follow the directions for your model; if you do not, continue to step 3.

❸ Pour sorbet mixture into a large baking dish or deep sheet pan. Cover dish or pan with aluminum foil and place in freezer for 3-4 hours, until nearly frozen solid. If you'd prefer, you may serve the sorbet at this stage by running an ice cream scoop down the length of the dish to scrape together a nice, full scoop. For an even more solid, yet still creamy consistency, continue to step 4.

❹ Use a metal spatula to scrape the nearly frozen sorbet out of the pan in large chunks. Place these chunks back into the Master Prep™ Pro Pitcher. Secure the Pitcher's top and pulse for 15 seconds, until extremely smooth and creamy. Transfer this finished sorbet mixture into any airtight container and freeze overnight before serving.

If serving to children: you can keep the creaminess and lose the alcohol by dissolving ¼ of a packet of watermelon flavored gelatin into the sugar and water mixture in step 1. Only let cool for 5 minutes instead of 20, stirring occasionally, as gelatin lumps may form.

Pro **Pitcher**

Lemon **Sorbet**

Lemon sorbet is probably the most popular flavor of sorbet in the world. The balance between the tart lemon and sweet sugar makes it absolutely irresistible.

Directions

❶ Place sugar and water in a sauce pan over medium heat, stirring constantly, just until sugar dissolves. Let cool for 20 minutes.

Shopping **List**

1 cup sugar

1 cup water

1 cup lemon juice

zest of 1 minute

Serves **3**

❷ Place cooled sugar mixture and all remaining ingredients in the Master Prep™ Pro Pitcher. Secure the Pitcher's top and pulse for 20 seconds, until zest is finely chopped. If you own an ice cream maker, stop here and follow the directions for your model; if you do not, continue to step 3.

❸ Pour sorbet mixture into a large baking dish or deep sheet pan. Cover dish or pan with aluminum foil and place in freezer for 3-4 hours, until nearly frozen solid. If you'd prefer, you may serve the sorbet at this stage by running an ice cream scoop down the length of the dish to scrape together a nice, full scoop. For an even more solid, yet still creamy consistency, continue to step 4.

❹ Use a metal spatula to scrape the nearly frozen sorbet out of the pan in large chunks. Place these chunks back into the Master Prep™ Pro Pitcher. Secure the Pitcher's top and pulse for 15 seconds, until extremely smooth and creamy. Transfer this finished sorbet mixture into any airtight container and freeze overnight before serving.

Make a tangerine sorbet by substituting 1 cup of freshly squeezed tangerine juice in place of the lemon juice, and the zest of 1 tangerine in place of the lemon zest.

ice creams

Pro **Pitcher**

Coffee Granita

Granitas and sorbets are both types of Italian ice and share the same basic ingredients (a water based ingredient and sugar), but granitas are typically coarser and chunkier than sorbet. This coffee flavored granita couldn't be any easier, made with only coffee and sugar. Serve drizzled with chocolate syrup for the best presentation.

Shopping **List**

1 ½ cups strong coffee
½ cup sugar
2 tablespoons water

Serves **2**

Directions

❶ Brew strong coffee (50% more coffee grounds than you would ordinarily brew with).

❷ Stir sugar into hot coffee until dissolved and then pour mixture into an ice cube tray. Freeze at least 4 hours, or until frozen solid.

❸ Place frozen coffee cubes in the Master Prep™ Pro Pitcher, secure the Pitcher's top and pulse in 7-10 long pulses, until grated.

❹ Add 2 tablepoons of water and pulse 2-3 more times before serving.

 If you don't mind the alcohol, a really wonderful treat is substituting 2-3 tablespoons of Kahlua in place of the water in step 4.

Bob Warden has forty years experience as a chef, restaurant owner, television personality, and kitchenware product developer. Well known as an on air kitchen presenter at QVC, Bob has helped develop over 1,000 kitchen products for the network. His previous cookbooks include *Best of the Best Cook's Essentials Cookbook* and *Bob Warden's Slow Food Fast*. Most of all, Bob Warden loves to cook and experiment in the kitchen.

RECIPE INDEX ⦿⦿⦿⦿⦿⦿⦿⦿⦿